SELF LOVE MAGIC

AN EMBODIED JOURNEY HOME TO YOURSELF

IRIS BEAGLEHOLE

Copyright © 2025 by Iris Beaglehole

All rights reserved.

No part of this book may be reproduced in any form or by any electronic or mechanical means, including information storage and retrieval systems, without written permission from the author, except for the use of brief quotations in a book review.

This book is dedicated to you, brave soul, ready to break the spell and remember you were never the problem…

You were always the magic.

1

THE WOUND AND THE SPELL

You are enough...

Place your hand on your heart. Feel it beating beneath your palm. That steady rhythm has been with you since before you could think about it. Still going, despite everything that's happened. Sometimes that's all we need to remember, we're still here.

I want to tell you something that might sound impossible right now: you are not broken. You never were.

I know this might land like a sharp stone in the tender place.

I used to feel so broken. Every morning I woke to an ache that had been there since late childhood. It drove me to the small rebellions of cigarettes behind the school buildings, to the fiercer addiction of infatuation - that drug that promises to fill every empty place if only you can lose yourself completely enough.

The pain was real. The wound was real, and yet underneath it all, I was still whole. I believe the same is likely true for you.

I understand if these words feel impossible when the pain is so real, so present, so overwhelming

Think of a tree that's been struck but remains standing. The wound is painful. Perhaps it even changes how the tree grows. Over time, the bark slowly covers what was raw. The tree carries its story in its shape, but nature heals. It keeps living. We look at the tree and see the scars, yes, but we don't say it's broken. We see how it lives, how it grows. Scar tissue is stronger than ordinary skin.

Sometimes, when we've been wounded, we feel broken, and the old emotion around our wounds keeps us in that pain. It can feel strange to be told you are not broken when the ache still lingers, unhealed.

Perhaps you've spent years convinced of your fundamental wrongness. I know how it feels to carry it in your bones, this fear that you're flawed at the core. Not just that you've done wrong things, but that you *are* wrong. That your very existence requires apology.

I know because I lived under that spell for so long I forgot there was any other way to be. The labels came early and stuck like burrs: selfish, lazy, too sensitive, unreliable. I absorbed them into my bloodstream. By the time I could form thoughts about myself, the thoughts were already poisoned. This was compounded by not being naturally very good at a lot of things like sports or anything involving co-ordination! I wasn't particularly good at school unless something lit me up from the inside. I had no confidence. I didn't know how to trust the voice inside me.

After years of untangling this mess, I've discovered we are all living under an enchantment that is doing us no good.

If you're holding this book, some part of you is ready to stop the war with yourself and ready to discover what happens when you choose yourself instead of abandoning yourself.

This readiness might not feel like readiness. It might feel like exhaustion, you simply can't keep up the performance anymore. It might feel like desperation. It might even feel like rebellion, a quiet "no" rising from somewhere in your bones.

You don't need to believe in magic. You don't need to have it all figured out. You don't even need to like yourself yet. All those requirements that usually come with self-help, forget them. You just need a spark of willingness. The tiniest flame of hope that things could be different. I've seen people transform their entire relationship with themselves starting with nothing more than "I'm tired of feeling this way."

The Spell We're Under

It's the spell of perpetual inadequacy, woven so tightly into the fabric of our culture that we mistake it for reality. This spell gnaws at us constantly: You must earn your worth. You must perfect yourself before you deserve love. You must be exceptional but not threatening, successful but not intimidating. The contradictions alone could drive you mad.

We breathe this spell in with our first breath. It seeps through family systems where love was scarce and had to be earned through performance. Where affection came with strings attached. Where belonging meant being good enough, smart enough, helpful enough, invisible enough. It comes from billboards and screens selling us solutions to problems we didn't know we had. It echoes in classrooms where worth gets measured in grades, where we learn early that we are only as valuable as our latest achievement.

The spell has many names. Some people call it perfectionism. Some people call it capitalism or patriarchy. Each system reinforces the others. Underneath them all is the same message, you are not enough as you are. You must constantly strive, improve, optimise. Rest is laziness. Contentment is complacency. Self-worth must be earned through pleasing everyone else.

And we believe it. We believe it so deeply that we can't imagine any other way of being.

Living under this spell costs us everything. We lose connection to our bodies, treating them as machines to optimise. We push through exhaustion, ignore hunger, override pain. We evaluate our bodies like merchandise, too much here, not enough there, always requiring improvement. We forget that our bodies are not projects. They're the vessels of our aliveness.

We lose trust in our emotions, seeing them as inconveniences. Anger becomes dangerous, something to suppress rather than a signal that boundaries have been crossed. Sadness becomes weakness. Even joy becomes suspect; too much happiness and people might think we're naive. We learn to perform acceptable emotions while the real ones rot inside us.

We struggle to have authentic relationships because we can't show up as ourselves when we believe we're fundamentally flawed. We curate our personalities like social media feeds. We bond over shared complaints rather than genuine connection. We hide our struggles until they become too big to contain, then feel ashamed when we finally break.

Most painfully, we lose the actual experience of being alive. We're so busy trying to earn our place here that we forget we were born belonging. We miss sunsets while planning tomorrow's productivity. We rush through meals while reading about optimal nutrition. The spell keeps us focused on a future where we'll finally be enough, stealing the only moment we actually have.

When I say you're not broken, I'm not engaging in wishful thinking. I'm pointing to something real, your original wholeness that exists beneath all the wounds.

Think of a tree that grows bent because of the prevailing wind. It's not broken. It's adapted. It's survived. Its essential tree-ness remains intact. You are like that tree. Whatever shaped you, whatever forces bent you, your essence remains whole. The ways you learned to protect yourself, to make yourself small or acceptable. These aren't character flaws. They're proof of your ability to survive.

The Origins of the Wound

For most of us, the wound begins early. Maybe it was the moment a parent's face showed disappointment and you learned you could be "wrong." That flash of frustration or disgust that crossed their features when you were just being yourself. The first time someone told you that you were too much or not enough. Too loud, too sensitive, too demanding. Not quiet enough, not tough enough, not easy enough.

These moments accumulate. Each one teaches us to mistrust ourselves a little more. The wound isn't just personal, it's inherited. We absorb the unhealed pain of parents who were told they weren't enough, who passed that message on not from malice but from their own wounding. We inherit the fears of family systems where love was scarce, where belonging required betraying parts of yourself.

Sometimes the wound comes from broader systems, the teacher who said you'd never amount to anything, the culture that said your body was wrong, the society that demanded you fit into boxes too small to hold you. These wounds layer upon each other until we mistake them for our actual shape. Like a rose bush that must be pruned to bloom more magnificently, sometimes what feels uncomfortable to face and and cut away, is actually making space for new growth. The gardener's shears seem cruel, but come spring, the plant that was cut back severely often blooms most abundantly. This is not to suggest we cut off parts of ourselves, but that we release the old thoughts, stories, patterns and beliefs that no longer serve us, so that we can bloom again.

What the Spell Serves

That voice in your head telling you you're not good enough? It thinks it's helping.

The inner critic developed when you were young and needed to figure out how to stay safe. If criticism helped you avoid punishment, your psyche internalised it. If being perfect kept you from rejection, your inner critic became a perfectionist. Understanding this doesn't mean we let it run the show. But it helps to know it's not your enemy, it's a protector using outdated methods.

Who benefits from you believing you're not enough?

Industries that profit from selling you solutions to manufactured flaws. The diet industry needs you to hate your body. The beauty industry requires your insecurity. People often try to sell you something based on undermining you, telling you that you aren't enough and need fixing.

Relationships that require your self-abandonment benefit from your lack of self love: the friend who needs you small so they can feel big, the partner who benefits from your self-doubt, the family dynamics that only function if you play your assigned role.

Your self-doubt is profitable. Your self-hatred is convenient. Your belief in your inadequacy keeps you controllable. Think about it: if you really knew you were already whole and worthy, what would you stop buying? What would you stop tolerating? What would you start demanding?

The moment we stop believing we're broken, we become dangerous to the status quo.

The Body Knows

As you read this, what's happening in your body?

You might notice tightness in your chest, the words you've swallowed. A clenching in your belly, the way you've learned to brace against criticism. Heaviness in your limbs, the exhaustion of carrying this weight. Or maybe numbness, the way you've learned to leave when things get too real.

Whatever you're experiencing is information. That chronic shoulder tension? Might be the weight of impossible expectations. That knot in your stomach? Years of swallowed anger. That feeling of disconnection? Maybe the only way you knew to survive.

Your body has been keeping score all along. It remembers every moment you abandoned yourself, every time you overrode your needs, every instance you chose external approval over internal truth. It's waiting for you to finally listen.

If you're feeling resistance, grief, anger, or even hope, good. These feelings mean the spell is starting to break.

Leonard Cohen sang about the crack in everything, how that's where the light gets in. Your awareness of the spell is the crack. Your willingness to question it is the light.

If that critical voice is loud right now, instead of fighting it, speak to it like you would a scared animal. "Thank you for trying to protect me. I hear you. I've got this now. You can rest."

Notice what happens when you offer this gentleness. Does something soften? Does something resist? There's no right response, only information about where you are right now.

Breaking the Spell

When the spell begins to lift, and it will, slowly, something extraordinary happens. You don't become a different person. You remember who you always were beneath the layers of conditioning.

You start to feel a different quality of tiredness, the good exhaustion from living your actual life instead of performing it. Your voice finds its natural register. Your shoulders remember how to rest.

Relationships shift. Some deepen as you show up more fully. Others fall away, they required your self-abandonment to function. You find yourself saying no without elaborate justifications. You say yes to things that previously felt selfish, rest, pleasure, creative expression, simply being.

The inner critic doesn't disappear. It transforms from a tyrant to a worried friend you can comfort. The shame doesn't vanish. It loosens its grip, becoming weather passing through rather than your permanent climate.

This becomes possible when you decide you're worthy of your own regard. Right now. Not when you're perfect. Not when you've fixed yourself. In all your messy humanity.

The spell breaks the moment you start questioning it. What if I'm not broken? What if I don't need to earn love? What if I'm already enough?

These questions are revolutionary. They challenge everything you've been taught. Every time you catch the critic in action, every time you notice yourself trying to earn worth, every time you choose tenderness over harshness, you're unravelling the spell.

The work ahead isn't about becoming someone new. It's about remembering who you were before the world convinced you that you needed to be different. It's gathering up the parts you've hidden, rejected, forgotten.

We'll move slowly. Those defences kept you safe. We honour them even as we begin to let them go. You've been under this spell for years. Of course it takes time to find your way out.

The fact that you're reading this means the work has already begun. That remembering isn't always comfortable. Sometimes it feels like grief for the years lost to self-hatred. Sometimes like rage at those who planted these seeds of shame. Sometimes like terror at the prospect of being seen without your armour.

All of it is welcome. All of it is part of your return.

Some days you'll feel progress. Other days you'll feel back at the beginning. Both are true. Both are necessary. You don't have to believe you're loveable yet. You don't have to feel ready. You just have to be willing to consider that maybe the voices that told you that you were wrong... were wrong.

That's enough. That crack in your certainty about your unworthiness, that's where the light gets in.

When you're ready, we'll continue with something manageable: learning to approve of yourself. Basic approval. Being on your own side.

It changes more than you might think.

Reclaiming Your Story Medicine

We are story-telling beings. From the moment we can understand language, we're swimming in narrative: fairy tales at bedtime, myths on movie screens, the stories our families tell about who we are and where we come from. These function as instruction manuals for being human, maps of the psyche, blueprints for what's possible and what's forbidden.

Clarissa Pinkola Estés taught us to read these stories differently, seeing them as more than relics from a simpler time, understanding them as living medicine. In her excavations of old tales, she shows us that fairy tales are diagnostic tools: they reveal where we're stuck and prescribe the cure. They show us that what we're experiencing goes beyond personal failure into archetypal passage. Others have been lost in this dark forest before. Others have found their way out.

We've been fed corrupted versions of these tales. The stories that could heal us have been sanitised, moralised, twisted to serve the very systems that wound us.

We all know the story of Cinderella. In the Disney version, she's rescued by a prince, her worth confirmed by his choice. In older versions, she speaks to her dead mother through a tree, she has agency and magic, she actively creates her transformation. The birds that help her symbolise her connection to the wild, instinctual self.

We internalise the cleaned-up version: *Wait prettily and someone will save you.* We miss the medicine of the older tale: *Your mother-line has power. Nature conspires to help you. You already have everything you need. You aren't just the princess, you are the prince too. In the end, we need to save ourselves from our own inner critical parts that seek control and destruction..*

In the inner world that reflects the narratives and stories of our culture, we are all the characters. The inconsistencies in fairytales and mythology used to bother me until I discovered that all these things do indeed make sense in the inner world of dreams and imagination. The secret teaching hidden in every fairy tale reveals that we are not just the protagonist. We are every character in the story. Estés calls this "the interior drama", recognising that each figure represents an aspect of our own psyche.

Little Red Riding Hood teaches us about predators, though differently than expected. Yes, there are real wolves in the world who would devour innocence. The wolf also represents our own hunger, our own wildness, our own sharp teeth that we've been taught to hide.

The story splits the feminine into parts: the too-young girl, the old grandmother, and the wolf who would eat them both. What if they're all aspects of one psyche? The innocent part trying to reach the wise part, and the wild part that's been cast out and turned predatory from starvation?

The huntsman who cuts open the wolf's belly to free the grandmother and child is more than an external rescuer. He's the part of us that can take decisive action, that can cut through the devouring patterns to liberate what's been swallowed.

When we read stories this way, they stop being cautionary tales about stranger danger and become maps for integration. The wolf represents more than external threat, embodying the part of us that's been starved of authentic expression, turned predatory in its exile.

In Hans Christian Andersen's earlier retelling of The Little Mermaid folk tale (long before Disney made it palatable) a young woman literally gives up her voice to walk in a world that's not hers, every step like knives. She endures agony and muteness for the chance at love, and in the original, she doesn't even get the prince. She dissolves into foam.

How many of us have lived this story? Trading our voice for access to worlds that require our silence? Walking through life in pain, unable to speak our truth, hoping our sacrifice will be rewarded with belonging?

Andersen, himself knew about trading voice for acceptance. As a man who loved men in 19th century Denmark, he poured his unspoken longings into stories, particularly this one which he was known to have written after the man he was in love with married a woman. Under this lens, the perspective deepens. The Little Mermaid becomes even more poignant when we see it as a story of queer silence - the agony of walking in a world that demands you suppress your true nature, every step like knives. How many have given up their authentic voice to move through spaces that allow only acceptable desires? The mermaid's dissolution into foam mirrors the hopeless despair we feel when when we cannot speak our truth.

Even this tragic tale holds medicine. The mermaid becomes a spirit of the air, finding immortality beyond the prince's love via her own suffering transformed into compassion. She finds a different kind of immortality, one born from her own journey rather than another's validation. The story, read deeply, says: even if you've given up your voice, even if you're walking on knives, transformation is still possible. The prince won't be your source.

In Sleeping Beauty the entire kingdom falls under the spell. Everyone goes unconscious. The hedge of thorns grows thick. Time stops. The sense of self disassociates and goes dormant until that active part of the psyche can emerge. And the prince? He's not the first to try. The hedge is littered with the bones of those who attempted to break through before the time was right. The curse has its own timeline. Some spells resist breaking by force or will, only yielding at the right moment with the right readiness. How long have you been asleep to your own life? What kingdom of possibility lies dormant within you? And what if the prince is just another aspect of yourself: the part finally ready to push through the thorns of old defences to wake what's been sleeping?

Estés invites us to do more than read stories, to dive into them, find where we live in them, use them as maps for our own becoming. The stories we were raised on, both the fairy tales and the cultural myths of success, beauty, worthiness, have shaped us more than we know. They live in our bodies as patterns, expectations, templates for what's possible. The princess waiting in the tower becomes the woman waiting for someone to choose her. The wicked stepmother becomes the inner voice that criticises. The poisoned apple becomes the toxic beliefs we swallow.

We can retell these stories. We can excavate the older versions, the wilder versions, the versions with teeth and transformation. We can recognise that we are every character, every element, and therefore we hold all the power needed for our own liberation.

As you write your origin story, consider:

- What fairy tales did you love or fear as a child?
- What characters did you identify with? Which ones frightened you?
- What stories did your family tell about who you are?
- What cultural myths have you swallowed whole?
- What character are you playing in your current life story?
- What character wants to emerge?

Remember: in the old stories, transformation often requires a journey through the dark forest, a descent to the underworld, an encounter with what seems monstrous. The maiden must lose her hands before she grows new ones of silver. The girl must wear the coat of rushes before her true nature is revealed. The hero must fail before they succeed.

Your wounds become initiations. Your struggles don't mean you're doing it wrong, rather, they're proof you're immersed in the heart of your own fairy tale, approaching the place where transformation lives. The question is, are you ready to wake up to your own power within this story? To no longer be the victim who is the innocent bystander in her own life, but to step into the role of creator, of main character?

The question is, are you living a story that serves your becoming? And if not, are you ready to remember that you're both the main character and the storyteller?

2

THE FIRST SPELL, I APPROVE OF MYSELF

The Impossible Words

There are words that can feel impossible in our mouths. "I love myself" might be one of them, too big, too bright, too foreign on a tongue trained in self-criticism. When we try to speak these words from a place of deep self-rejection, they can feel like lies, and our bodies know it. The resistance rises like bile, the internal voice laughs or sneers or simply goes numb.

This is honesty, not failure. And honesty is where all real change begins.

So we start smaller, quieter, with words that can slip past the guards at the gate of our disbelief. We begin with approval, that modest, revolutionary act of being on our own side.

My Journey: From Grandiose to Grounded

My journey with affirmations started in 2005 when I was twenty-one. A friend took me to visit an elderly woman called Mary who taught and practiced reiki. We sat in Mary's rose garden drinking tea while she told me about a book that had changed her life, *You Can Heal Your Life* by Louise Hay. The book was published in 1984 which happens to be the year I was born.

I took that book and worked with it for ten years. Really worked with it. Affirmations became my daily practice, my religion almost. I'd stand in front of mirrors declaring "I'm amazing and magnificent and all my dreams are coming true." I wrote affirmations in journals, on sticky notes, anywhere I could see it. I kept a notebook of affirmations that I liked, most of which I had written myself using the philosophy that they ought to be positive and make me feel good. I would find time throughout the day to sit with my notebook and go through them, noting how each made me feel.

This worked. I started to feel much better. With affirmations, I could induce waves of euphoria and I stopped considering myself depressed, although I still had some emotional instability throughout my twenties. I could be euphoric one minute and despairing the next with hardly any in-between.

The affirmations did rewire much of my social conditioning. Actively saying "I love myself" built up self-esteem where there had been none. The repetition carved new grooves in my brain, countering years of criticism. I became more confident, more willing to take risks, more able to see my own worth.

After a decade of this practice, I hit a wall. The affirmations could only take me so far. When I wasn't feeling good, telling myself I was "magnificence in human form" felt like gaslighting myself. The disconnect between what I was saying and what I was experiencing created its own kind of pain. I'd affirm my amazingness while feeling like garbage, and the gap between those two realities became another source of shame.

There was still more foundational work to do, work that grand affirmations couldn't touch.

By 2015, I was drowning in the pressure to be AMAZING, special, wonderful, outstanding. The self-help world kept insisting I reach for the stars, manifest magnificence, become my most extraordinary self. I was exhausted from all that striving toward an impossible ideal. The affirmations that once felt empowering now felt like another way I was failing, I couldn't even positive-think my way to happiness correctly.

Then a quieter truth emerged: "I'm good enough."

The phrase felt almost embarrassingly simple. Where was the sparkle? The transformation? But as I sat with it, something settled in my chest.

'I'm good enough' is a solid foundation.

It's digestible, I realised. It's believable. It's no great commitment, no great pressure. It's acceptable, and it's honest.

When my daughter was young, I struggled with a big flare up of Chronic Fatigue Syndrome. I sometimes struggled to get out of bed, let alone play with a three year old. I always made sure her basic needs were met, and I had some support, but I couldn't be everything she wanted me to be all the time. I couldn't be a whole village. My sassy American therapist, Sherry, with the white streak in her perfectly coiffed hair told me there was nothing wrong with being a good-enough mother. Donald Winnicott, who developed this concept, understood that 'good enough' holds more grace than perfect ever could. As human beings we cannot be perfect, but we can be enough. I could be a good-enough daughter, and granddaughter too, a good enough friend, a good-enough writer.

Enough became a calm centre in the storm of vulnerability and impossible expectations. Good enough was, finally, enough.

The Science and the Paradox

Sometimes when people attempt affirmations, they aim for the stars. They tell themselves how stunning and amazing and talented they are, and while there's nothing wrong with that, if they don't really believe it, it won't work. If you're carrying around negative messages about yourself, consciously or unconsciously, then those wonderful positive things can't take root in hostile soil.

The research on self-affirmations, dating back to Claude Steele's work in 1988, shows they work by affirming self-worth through reflection on core values. This gives people a broader view of themselves beyond their usual mental limits. The key finding is that affirmations work best when they connect to our values and feel believable, not when they're aspirational fantasies.

More recent research on neuroplasticity confirms that repetition of a new practice, thought or idea can create new neural pathways. These pathways form most effectively when there's resonance between what we are saying and what we can connect with, value and trust. Grand declarations can sometimes create cognitive dissonance whereas small, believable statements slip past our defences, planting in our unconscious minds where they can sprout and take root and grow into better feeling thoughts and patterns.

My psychologist friend Zoe helped me understand a deeper issue: the paradox at the heart of self-help. We're expected to fix everything ourselves, to bootstrap our way to wellness through individual effort and positive thinking. Yet we evolved as communal animals. Our survival depended on connection, mutual support, tight-knit groups that looked after each other.

The self-help industry takes our collective wounds and sells us individualistic solutions. It's deeply capitalistic in its approach, always pushing for more abundance, more manifestation, more optimization. If you're struggling, the message is clear: you must not be doing the inner work correctly. This becomes especially cruel when applied to people dealing with chronic illness, systemic discrimination, poverty, or disability.

So how do we use tools like affirmations without falling into the trap of believing we can positive-think our way out of systemic problems? We can work with the tension of the paradox.

There is power in paradox. When we hold two opposing truths at once, it creates space where there seemed to be none. Like a plant growing through concrete, something new emerges when we refuse to collapse into either side. We can tend our childhood wounds while also knowing that poverty isn't a personal failing. We can practice self-love despite the injustice in the world.

When we stop trying to make the tension go away, we find it has something to teach us. The real power comes when we hold both truths: Yes, our thoughts matter and shape our experience. And yes, we need actual support, resources, and collective action to address many of life's challenges.

Your Body Already Knows

Despite all my work on re-wiring my brain patterns with humble affirmations, the work continues to this day. Ten years ago I sat with my journal, excavating years of limiting beliefs. As I wrote "I approve of myself" my body told me everything I needed to know about my relationship with self-acceptance.

My jaw clenched. My shoulders crept toward my ears. My stomach tightened as if bracing for impact. This wasn't just mental resistance, it was a full-body rejection of the possibility that I might be acceptable as is. The inner critic roared: "Approve of WHAT exactly? Your failures? Your mistakes? The way you're behind on everything? The way you never follow through?" These kinds of reactions are information revealing where the wound lives and what needs healing.

When you practice approval, your body will tell you stories. Tightness in your throat might be old words of criticism lodged there. Heaviness in your chest could be grief for all the years of self-rejection. That churning in your stomach? Fear of what happens if you stop punishing yourself. Numbness or dissociation means your nervous system is protecting you from feeling too much too fast.

These aren't signs to stop. They're signs that something important is happening.

The resistance to self-approval is a protector that's been working overtime. It learned early that self-criticism might keep you safe from external criticism. That staying small might prevent rejection. That punishing yourself first meant others couldn't hurt you as badly.

So when you sit down to write "I approve of myself" and every part of you rebels, work with it, not against it. Thank the resistance for trying to protect you. Get curious about its fears. What would happen if you approved of yourself? Will you become lazy? Selfish? Delusional? These fears are usually old messages from childhood dressed up as wisdom.

When resistance arises, breathe into the sensation. Put your hand where you feel it, on your body. Rock gently. Hum. Move. Let your body process what your mind is struggling with. Your wonderful brain has concocted patterns to keep you functioning, and even though some might be harmful, they're deeply entrenched and will resist change.

The Practice: A Direct Approach

Now, it's going to get messy, just like cleaning a roasting pan looks worse before it gets better. Every time you change something in your life, you deal with resistance and the sediment that gets kicked up. Just as gardening requires dealing with dirt, changing thought patterns means dealing with the mess.

Take your notebook. Find a pen that flows easily. We're going to start simple.

Write at the top of your page: "I approve of myself."

How does that feel? Take a moment to reflect. Now write it again, at least ten times:

I approve of myself

I approve of myself

I approve of myself

I approve of myself

I approve of myself

I approve of myself

I approve of myself

I approve of myself

I approve of myself

I approve of myself

Notice your reactions without judgment. Does it feel true? Like a lie? Do you want to argue with it? Good. You're at the beginning, and that's where we start.

If you are struggling with approval, take a step back and focus instead on acceptance. Drop the need to try. Drop the effort. Drop into acceptance. Can you accept that you are a human being living in this complex world, doing your best to do your best?

How does it feel to write and say aloud"

I accept myself

I accept myself

I accept myself

I accept myself, exactly as I am.

I have no control over what has come before, but I accept that it has happened. I accept that I am here now.

Now continue. Fill a whole page, or five, or ten. Write it over and over, noting any thoughts or feelings of resistance that come up, but not dwelling on them.

When you've written the affirmation at least fifty times, things begin to shift. Eventually, a small voice says "what if this could be true?"

After writing, try reading it aloud to yourself. Pay attention to how you feel. You'll probably feel silly, resistant, hopeful, angry, all normal responses as you rewire thought patterns.

Take this practice everywhere. Repeat it as you're going to bed, as you're walking or driving, as you cook, as you eat. Write it on your bathroom mirror. Put it where you'll see it. Repeat it until you find yourself thinking it unconsciously.

Before checking your phone each morning, place your hand on your heart and say "I approve of myself." Feel your heartbeat. You're approving of a living, breathing human who deserves basic kindness.

When you notice self-criticism arising, pause. Take three breaths. Say "I accept myself even as I struggle with this." You're not necessarily approving of the behaviour, you're approving of your being, even in all the struggles you experience, just as you'd approve of a dear friend going through similar struggles.

When you practice approval consistently, things shift in unexpected ways. Your inner dialogue changes first. The voice that used to say "You idiot" might say "Oops, let's try again." As you trust yourself more, the catastrophising lessens and you're less defensive because you're not constantly bracing for your own attacks.

Approval as Foundation

Approval is the first spell because it creates the conditions for everything else. You can't meet your shadow with compassion if you're attacking yourself. You can't reclaim your brilliance if you believe you deserve dimness. You can't inhabit your body with respect if you're treating it as a problem.

Think of approval as tilling the soil. It prepares the ground for deeper self-love to take root. It creates enough internal safety for the more vulnerable work ahead. As you continue this practice, you might notice old griefs arising that need tending. Parts of yourself you've exiled might start asking to come home. Your body might begin to trust you enough to feel. Desires you'd forgotten you had might stir.

This is the ice melting. The ground softening. Your system is beginning to believe that maybe, possibly, you're on your own side.

Affirmations without integration can become another form of self-abandonment. If we use "I approve of myself" to bypass genuine hurt or avoid necessary grief, we're just creating a shinier cage. True approval includes approving of your resistance to approval, your messy feelings, your imperfect journey, your very human struggles, your need for support, your right to take time.

We start with "I approve of myself" rather than "I love myself" because approval has room for the full spectrum. It says: "I see all of this, the light and shadow, the progress and regression, the clarity and confusion, and I choose to be on my own side through it all."

Self-love doesn't arrive fully formed. It grows slowly, the way all real things grow. It can begin with this simple, radical act of approval, this choosing to be on your own side. You don't have to love yourself yet. You just have to be willing to stop being your own enemy.

The Feeling is the Spell

Your feeling is what matters most with affirmations. The words themselves are just tools, like tuning forks that help you find the right frequency. When an affirmation rings true in your body, when it creates a sensation or resonance you can feel, that's when the magic happens. You're tuning in to the energetic vibration of what you want to experience.

Our ancestors understood this. They shaped sound into story and rhyme, chant and mantra and song, to remember, share understand and shape their worlds. They knew that words carry energy, and that energy needs to move through you, not just sit in your logical mind. If you say an affirmation only with your conscious thoughts, you're just telling yourself a story, and your mind will probably argue with it. The mind loves to argue with stories. Feel into the words instead:

Love, family, friendship, community, compassion, trust, connection, intimacy.

Learning, growth, wisdom, creativity, courage, integrity, awareness.

Purpose, excellence, leadership, innovation, service, achievement, recognition, success.

Freedom, independence, authenticity, autonomy, spontaneity.

Security, health, safety, stability, balance, peace, comfort, generosity.

Joy, adventure, pleasure, humour, vitality, gratitude, beauty.

Truth, justice, equality, nature, spirituality, simplicity, faith.

Run your attention over these words, feeling the resonance of each one. Which ones stand out to you? So any feel sharp or wrong? If so, you could gently feel into what lies beneath.

Do any of these words really sing to you? Make a list to keep track of in your journal (or if you are not into journaling, feel free to draw or create a song or something else that does work for you).

I recommend becoming a collector of beautiful words, wherever you find them. Hold these words, one by one. Let them open something in you. Do they have a colour when you say them? A flavour? Do they create any kind of sensation in your body? If a particular word feels wrong or creates resistance, choose a different one. Scan through different words until you find ones that make sense for your particular system.

There's an important balance to understand here; when you put an intention out into the cosmos with an affirmation, you're doing the active part. You're sending out your signal. But for it to work, you also need to line up with the receptive part in order to be open to receive what you're calling in. Think of it as both broadcasting and tuning your receiver to the same station. You're putting the idea out while simultaneously creating space to recognise and welcome it when it arrives.

Feeling matters the most. When you feel the truth of an affirmation in your body, you naturally align with it. You become a clear conduit for what you're inviting into your life.

Why Mirrors Reveal Everything

When Louise Hay, the godmother of self-help first stood before her bathroom mirror in the 1970s and tried to say "I love you" to her reflection, she burst into tears. This wasn't the reaction of someone who'd had an easy life. By then, she'd survived a childhood of abuse and extreme poverty, pregnant and abandoned at sixteen. She'd escaped all that, or so she'd thought: reinvented herself as a fashion model in New York, married a businessman who left her after fourteen years for another woman, and started a new life with a focus on helping people only to face a diagnosis of cancer.

She still had a lot of deep healing to do. The mirror reflected back every wound, every moment she'd been taught she was worthless. When she tried to meet her own eyes with love, her body recoiled. Sometimes she could only manage a few seconds. Sometimes the only part of her body she could compliment were her eyebrows! Sometimes she wanted to smash the glass. But she kept returning, understanding intuitively what neuroscience would later confirm: repetition creates new neural pathways. If she could learn self-hatred through repetition, she could learn self-love the same way.

Mirror work, the practice of looking at yourself while speaking affirmations, became central to Hay's teaching because it's impossible to hide from yourself in a mirror. You can write affirmations in a journal without feeling them. You can say them while driving without connecting. But when you look into your own eyes and speak, every resistance surfaces. That's precisely the point.

Mirrors are symbolic of reflections and revelation. The mirror triggers us because it reflects not just our physical appearance but our entire relationship with ourselves. Every criticism we've internalised lives in how we see our reflection. Every time we scan for flaws instead of beauty, we're reenacting old patterns of rejection. The practice interrupts this unconscious cruelty, replacing it with something so foreign it feels like lying: kindness toward ourselves.

Hay's genius was understanding that the feeling of falseness didn't matter. "Of course it feels like lying," she would tell her clients. "If you believed, you wouldn't need the practice." She compared it to planting seeds, you don't dig them up daily to check if they're growing. You trust the process, water them with consistency, and give them time.

She also understood that mirror work had to meet people where they were. For those who couldn't say "I love you," to themselves in the mirror, she suggested starting with "I'm willing to learn to like you" or even just "Hello, I see you." For those who couldn't look at their faces, she recommended starting with one feature, maybe your hands, maybe your eyes, maybe just your shadow on the wall. The point wasn't perfection but presence.

What made Hay's approach radical wasn't just the affirmations, it was the insistence on staying present with whatever arose. When clients reported crying at the mirror, she celebrated it. The tears meant something was moving. When they felt rage, she saw it as the anger finally having somewhere to go instead of turning inward. Every resistance was information, every emotion a teacher.

Louise went on to live a long, inspiring and beautiful life, bringing joy to many people. She learned to ballroom dance in her 80s. She'd always wanted to, as a child, but had been told she was too tall. This just goes to show that it's never too late to learn and explore the things that light you up. May we all be as radiant and vibrant and willing to try new things as Louise Hay at 80 years of age!

The Practice of Staying Present

Mirror work isn't about convincing yourself of something false. It's about making space for something true that's been buried under conditioning. When you look at yourself with soft eyes, what psychologists call the "facial feedback hypothesis", your nervous system receives signals of safety. When you speak kindly to your reflection, you're creating what therapists call a "corrective emotional experience," offering yourself the loving gaze you may never have received.

The deeper teaching is about not abandoning yourself when difficult emotions arise. Most of us have been leaving ourselves for years, dissociating when things get hard, numbing when pain surfaces, turning away from our own reflection both literally and metaphorically. Mirror work is a practice of return. You show up, speak your truth (even if that truth is just "this is hard"), and stay present with whatever happens.

To begin, choose one mirror you pass regularly, perhaps your bathroom mirror, and commit to just ten seconds of practice each time you're there. Start by simply meeting your own eyes without immediately looking away. When that feels manageable, add words. Begin with something neutral like "Hello, [your name]" or "I see you." If you notice yourself scanning for flaws, gently redirect your gaze to your eyes, the windows to the part of you that has nothing to do with appearance. When you're ready, try Hay's fundamental phrase: "I love and accept you exactly as you are." Say it even if, especially if, you don't believe it. If emotions arise, let them. If you need to cry, cry to your own reflection. If you feel ridiculous, acknowledge that too: "I feel ridiculous and I'm here anyway." The practice is not in feeling any particular way but in staying present with whatever arises, building the muscle of self-companionship one mirror moment at a time.

Every mirror in your life is an opportunity. The bathroom mirror in the morning, the car mirror at stoplights, shop windows you pass. Each reflection is a chance to practice the radical act of meeting yourself with kindness instead of criticism, presence instead of abandonment, truth instead of the old lies you learned to believe.

Start where you are. If you can't yet say "I love you," say "I'm learning." If you can't yet look at your face, look at your hand. If you feel nothing but resistance, honour that too, resistance means something is shifting, something that's been frozen is beginning to thaw. The mirror doesn't lie, but neither does it tell the whole truth. It shows one moment, one angle, one surface of a being who has survived everything and is still here, still willing to try, still deserving of their own love.

I Am Enough

This phrase is medicine for the endless striving that leaves us exhausted and still feeling incomplete. Notice it doesn't say perfect or amazing or the best. Just enough, that beautiful word that means sufficient, acceptable, allowed to exist.

When you first try saying "I am enough" or "I'm good enough," your mind might rebel immediately. Good enough for what? According to whom? The beauty is that it doesn't need qualifiers. You're not claiming to be good enough at your job or as a parent or in relationships. You're saying your existence itself is sufficient. You don't have to earn your place here.

Try it now: "I am enough." What happens in your body? Does your chest tighten? Do tears come? Does a voice start listing all your failures? That voice is old conditioning speaking. It's every red mark on every paper, every sigh of disappointment, every time you came up short in someone's eyes.

Keep saying it anyway. Don't argue with the critical voice, just plant something new beside it. Being good enough doesn't mean you stop growing. You can be sufficient and still learning. You can be enough and still healing. You can be acceptable and still make mistakes daily.

I Love Myself

This one's usually harder. Love feels enormous, absolute. If saying you're good enough is like giving yourself a respectful nod, saying you love yourself is like opening your arms for an embrace. Most of us never learned how to hold ourselves with that kind of tenderness.

When you resist these words, and you probably will, remember that love can be a decision before it's a feeling. You don't need to feel warmth flooding your body. Think of how you might love a difficult family member: imperfectly, with frustration sometimes, yet with an underlying commitment to their wellbeing. That's enough for now.

"I love myself" can start as intention. You're stating a willingness to learn what self-love means, to practice it especially when you don't feel it. Some days these words might come through gritted teeth. Other days with tears. Both count.

If it feels too much, soften it: "I'm learning to love myself." "I'm willing to love myself." Or get specific: "I love my hands that make things." "I love my stubbornness that got me through." "I love the part of me that keeps trying."

The biggest fear is often that self-love equals selfishness or narcissism, which simply isn't true. Narcissists actually suffer from a huge disconnection from self and are overcompensating with a false grand delusion of who they really are. Consider this: when you love yourself, you stop draining others for validation. You stop needing constant reassurance. You have more to give because you're not running on empty. Self-love creates capacity for genuine generosity.

I have been journalling "I love myself" for so long now that it is part of the background noise of my psyche. When I go to bed at night, I hear it echo in my mind. "I love myself" – a gentle, soothing reminder of self-care, of connection to my soul, of honouring this one wild and precious life, as Mary Oliver would put it. I'd much rather have this kind of message playing in the background of my psyche than any of the mean, cruel, limiting judgements I grew up with, wouldn't you?

I Love My Life

This might trigger the most resistance, especially when life is hard. How can you love a life that includes loss, disappointment, struggle? Here's the secret: loving your life doesn't mean loving every moment. It means recognising that this one life you have, difficult, imperfect, sometimes painful, belongs to you, and there's something valuable in that ownership.

"I love my life" doesn't deny problems or bypass grief. You can love your life while working to change things. You can love your life while grieving losses. The love is for the whole messy truth of being alive, not for some imaginary perfect version.

Start small if you need to. Maybe you can't love your whole life today. Can you love this morning's quiet? This text from a friend? This song? "I love my life" can begin with "I love this moment."

Using the magic of affirmations to banish negative self-talk

Scan through the following list of negative self-talk. Whenever a negative statement strikes a chord with you, focus on the affirmation to counter it. Write this down in your journal. Feel free to adapt it or replace it with a better one for you.

. . .

COMMON NEGATIVE SELF-TALK **and Affirmations to Counter It**

Scan through the common negative self-talk lines below. If any resonate with you, draw your attention to the countering affirmation.

- I'm not good enough. —> *I am enough exactly as I am.*
- I always mess things up. —> *I learn and grow from every experience.*
- I'm too old to change. —> *There are always opportunities to create the life I want.*
- Nobody likes me. —> *I am worthy of love and belonging.*
- I'll never succeed. —> *I am capable, and I trust my journey.*
- I'm a failure. —> *I am learning and evolving every day.*
- I can't do anything right. —> *I am doing my best, and that is enough.*
- I'm so stupid. —> *I am intelligent and resourceful.*
- I'm a burden to others. —> *My presence matters and brings value.*
- I don't deserve happiness. —> *I deserve joy, love, and fulfilment*
- I'll always be alone. —> *I am opening to meaningful, nourishing connections.*
- I shouldn't even try. —> *Taking action moves me closer to my goals.*
- I'm too sensitive. —> *My sensitivity is a strength and a gift.*
- I'm not as good as they are. —> *My path and gifts are unique and valuable.*

- I'm ugly. —> *I am unique and beautiful in my own way.*
- I'm so lazy. —> *I allow myself to rest and recharge when needed.*
- I'm hopeless. —> *I have hope and resilience within me.*
- I can't trust myself. —> *I am learning to trust my intuition and wisdom.*
- I'm worthless. —> *My worth is inherent and unchangeable.*
- I'll never get better. —> *I am healing and growing every day.*
- No one cares about me. —> *I am loved and cared for more than I realise.*
- I'm always in the way. —> *I have a right to take up space. I belong here.*
- I'm too much. —> *My fullness is welcome and needed.*
- I'm not talented enough. —> *My talents are valuable and worth sharing.*
- I ruin everything. —> *I handle challenges with grace and self-compassion and mistakes only help me to learn and grow.*
- I'm weak. —> *I am strong and resilient.*
- I'm broken. —> *I am whole, even in my healing.*
- I never finish anything. —> *I am capable of completing what matters to me.*
- I don't matter. —> *My life has purpose and meaning when I connect to what I value and welcome more of what I care about into my life.*
- I'm a disappointment. —> *Even though I have struggled, I forgive myself so that I can make space to be proud of who I am becoming.*
- I always say the wrong thing. —> *My voice matters and deserves to be heard.*
- I'm unlovable. —> *I am worthy of love exactly as I am.*

Nothing ever works out for me. —> *Good things are possible for me.*

- I'm a bad person. —> *I am doing my best.*
- I should have known better. —> *I forgive myself for not knowing what I didn't know.*
- I'm too broken to be fixed. —> *I am healing, growing, and transforming.*
- I'm too anxious to cope. —> *I can handle this moment, one breath at a time.*
- I'm a fraud. —> *I am authentic and enough just as I am.*
- I don't deserve good things. —> *I am deserving of all the blessings life has to offer.*
- I'm not important. —> *I matter, and my life makes a difference.*
- I'm too damaged. —> *My past does not define my worth or my future.*
- I'll never be happy. —> *Happiness is possible and within my reach.*
- I can't trust anyone. —> *I am learning to open my heart safely and wisely.*
- I can't cope with this. —> *I am strong enough to face this challenge.*
- I'm always behind. —> *I am exactly where I need to be right now.*
- I'm too awkward. —> *My uniqueness is my strength.*
- I'm a loser. —> *I am worthy and valuable, no matter what.*
- I'm too fat/skinny. —> *My body is worthy of love and respect.*
- I'm a waste of space. —> *I have a right to exist and take up space.*

- I shouldn't feel this way. —> *My feelings are valid and deserve compassion.*
- I'm not creative. —> *My creativity flows in its own perfect way.*
- I always let people down. —> *I do my best, and that is enough.*
- I don't belong anywhere. —> *I am connected, and I belong.*
- I'm too shy. —> *My quiet nature has its own power and wisdom.*
- I never get it right. —> *Every attempt brings me closer to growth.*
- I'm just not cut out for this. —> *I have everything I need, to learn and adapt.*
- I'm too emotional. —> *My emotions are a sign of my depth and humanity.*
- I'm too sensitive to handle life. —> *My sensitivity helps me feel and connect deeply.*
- I'm just a mess. —> *I am a human being, perfectly imperfect and growing.*
- I'm always overlooked. —> *I am moving towards being seen and valued.*
- I don't fit in. —> *I belong wherever I choose to be.*
- I'm a coward. —> *I am brave in ways that matter.*
- I'm boring. —> *I am unique and worthy of attention.*
- I'm too slow. —> *I honour my natural pace.*
- I'm selfish. —> *Taking care of my needs is healthy and necessary.*
- I'm bad at relationships. —> *I am learning to build loving connections.*
- I'm too needy. —> *My needs are valid and deserve to be heard.*

- I always make mistakes. —> *Mistakes are opportunities to learn.*
- I'm unworthy of respect. —> *I am worthy of respect and kindness.*
- I'm always anxious. —> *I can choose to feel a little more calm and centred in this moment with each slow breath.*
- I'm just too much to handle. —> *I am exactly enough as I am.*
- I can't get anything done. —> *I am capable of taking small steps forward.*
- I'm a bad parent/friend/partner. —> *I am doing my best with love and care.*
- I'm too negative. —> *I can choose to see possibilities and hope.*
- I'm not disciplined enough. —> *I can build habits gently, one step at a time.*
- I'm a quitter. —> *I am allowed to change direction and start again or stick it out depending on what's right for me.*
- I'm too damaged to be loved. —> *I am worthy of love in all my forms.*
- I'll never be as successful as others. —> *My path unfolds at its own perfect pace.*
- I'm not smart enough. —> *I am intelligent in my own unique way.*
- I'm always behind everyone else. —> *I am on my own timeline, and that's okay.*
- I'm not capable of change. —> *I am capable of evolving and transforming.*
- I'm just unlucky. —> *Good things are coming to me.*
- I always say stupid things. —> *I speak with sincerity and heart.*

◆ I'm not brave enough to try. —> *I have courage within me right now.*

◆ I'm too introverted. —> *My introversion is a beautiful part of who I am.*

◆ I'm too broken to be fixed. —> *I am whole and healing every day.*

◆ I'm not interesting. —> *My story matters, and I am interesting.*

◆ I don't have anything to offer. —> *I bring unique gifts to the world.*

◆ I'm a terrible person. —> *I am doing my best.*

◆ I'm too far gone. —> *It's never too late for me to heal and grow.*

◆ I'm worthless without achievements. —> *My worth is not defined by what I do but by who I am as a unique being who belongs here on this earth.*

◆ I'll never be confident. —> *Confidence grows as I practise self-belief.*

◆ I can't be happy until everything is perfect. —> *I can find peace and joy in this moment.*

◆ I'll always feel this way. —> *All feelings pass in time.*

◆ I'm nothing special. —> *I am unique, and that is special.*

◆ I'm ungrateful. —> *I can appreciate the good in my life.*

◆ I'm impossible to love. —> *I am lovable exactly as I am.*

◆ I'm doomed to repeat my mistakes. —> *I can choose new ways of being.*

◆ I'm an imposter. —> *I am qualified and capable.*

◆ I'm too behind to catch up. —> *I can start fresh at any time.*

◆ I'm always too late. —> *The right time for me is now.*

◆ I'm stuck. —> *I am capable of moving forward, step by step.*

◈ I'm beyond help. —> *Support and healing are always available to me.*

PUT *your hand on your heart, chest or belly and read the lines that stand out, once more. Which negative self-talk are you most familiar with inside your own mind? How does the counter-affirmation feel? Notice how this new possibility sits with you.*

If any of the words are jarring, close your eyes and notice what other information comes through. Where does the discomfort arise from? does it have an old story? Old pain? Old fear? Let those feelings come up so that they can release.

Play around with the positive affirmation, choosing new words until it is an incantation that resonates within you in a way that feels good and supportive.

3

DEVOTION IN DAILY LIFE

The way we move through our days reveals everything about how we treat ourselves. Each transition, each mundane task, each moment of waiting contains the seed of self-love, if we know how to tend it. Yet most of us rush through these opportunities, waiting for perfect conditions while our actual lives pass by untouched by kindness toward ourselves.

Many people believe self-love requires special circumstances: meditation retreats, uninterrupted morning hours, an already-healed heart. Meanwhile we scroll through breakfast comparing ourselves to strangers, multitask through conversations without presence, treat our daily routines as obstacles rather than opportunities for care. But this moment-to-moment devotion to ourselves transforms the life we already have.

The Neuroscience of Self-Love Rituals

Michael Norton's research in *The Ritual Effect* reveals something profound about how we can rewire our relationship with ourselves. Norton found that rituals, even simple, made-up ones, create measurable changes in emotional regulation and sense of control. The repetition builds what he calls a "Ritual Immune Response," a buffer against life's chaos.

The rituals don't need to be elaborate. Study participants who created personal rituals like stirring coffee counterclockwise three times showed the same benefits as those following ancient practices. When Norton and Francesca Gino studied grief rituals, participants who drew their feelings, tore up the paper, and sprinkled salt on the pieces recovered faster than control groups. The ritual gave them agency over their pain.

My friend Stephanie found one thing that worked: playing her dance playlist when she felt disconnected from herself. One song. Sometimes just thirty seconds of movement. Her body learned that music meant returning to herself, choosing connection over abandonment. No meditation cushion required.

This is what self-love looks like in practice, finding the smallest reliable way to turn toward yourself instead of away.

Put your phone down for a minute

Sherry Turkle's MIT research showed that we check our phones 96 times daily. Each check potentially triggers comparison, self-criticism, the sense that everyone else has figured out what we're failing at. Our devices fragment our attention and diminish what Turkle calls "the solitary self", our capacity to be alone without feeling lonely.

But what if we reclaimed these portals for self-love? What if we turn our phone into an ally. My wallpaper is a photo I took on an early morning flight on my way to a retreat with my dear friend, Chantal. It depicts the moon at sunrise over feathery clouds. I have experimented with apps that send random affirmation alerts like "You are loved" or "Take a breath." I have a playlist of favourite meditations and songs to play when the inner critic gets loud. think about what similar things might support you in your journey.

The moments after waking are especially vulnerable. Your brain exists in a theta state, creative, open, undefended. When we immediately check phones, we hand this precious state to whoever posted overnight. Instead, try five to ten minutes of sovereignty each morning. This is time to remember you exist separate from digital demands. Place your hand on your heart. Ask yourself what you need. Let your first act be self-connection, not comparison. During this time you can meditate, but it doesn't need to be any particular way. If your mind is too busy, try the reading meditation at the end of this book. If sitting still is frustrating, try walking slowly, feeling the sensations and centring yourself in your body.

When sitting with someone, remember this moment isn't permanent. They won't be here forever. This awareness can pull you from your phone back to presence. The same applies to moments with ourselves, this particular morning, this specific tired body, this exact emotional state. All temporary. All deserving of attention.

Food as Self-Love Practice

Every meal offers a chance to practice caring for ourselves, but I'm not talking about Instagram-worthy smoothie bowls. Real food self-love might be eating breakfast sitting down instead of standing over the sink. It might be asking your body what it actually wants instead of what you think you should eat. It might be saying a simple "thank you, body" before meals, not for looking any particular way, but for continuing to transform food into life.

Thich Nhat Hanh writes beautifully about mindful eating, but sometimes self-love looks like enjoying your sandwich while watching TV, just grateful you fed yourself today. The practice includes noticing when you eat to punish versus nourish. When you use food to stuff down feelings versus feel them. When you deny yourself pleasure because you don't think you deserve it.

This isn't just fantasy make-believe. Research shows that mindful eating improves digestion and satisfaction, but more importantly, it's a chance to practice receiving.

So many of us are terrible at receiving compliments, help, nourishment. Starting with consciously receiving food can teach us to receive in other ways too.

Sound and Movement as Self-Return

Alfred Tomatis's research shows certain frequencies literally reorganise our nervous systems. Humming creates vibrations that stimulate the vagus nerve, activating rest-and-digest responses. You don't need to chant in Sanskrit. Three minutes of humming in the shower can be an act of self-soothing, especially when anxiety rises.

Even environmental sounds, the refrigerator's hum, bird songs, distant traffic, can become anchors for self-connection when we listen with curiosity instead of irritation. The practice is using whatever's present to come back to ourselves.

Peter Levine observed that animals shake after trauma to discharge stress. We've socialised ourselves out of this natural reset. When I feel activated, I shake for one minute. It looks ridiculous. It works. My body gets to complete what my mind keeps cycling through.

Movement as self-love doesn't mean punishing workouts. When I'm in a good routine, I do five minutes of gentle yoga while the kettle boils, a few sun salutations, cat and cow stretches, then lying on my back to check in with myself. This is a small enough ritual that takes such a short time, meaning I don't skip it because I'm feeling rushed. I have to wait for that kettle to boil anyway, I might as well use the time to give myself the gift of stretching, and I know my back will thank me later in the day!

Even regular walking becomes self-love when you use it to practice approval. With each step: "I (step) approve (step) of (step) myself (step)." Your body might believe what it hears in rhythm more than what you say sitting still.

Daily Rituals for Real Life

- When you wake up, before your mind starts its list of failures and tasks, place your hand on your chest. Feel your heartbeat. Don't reach for your phone. Don't start planning. Just this small promise of alliance with yourself. Say affirmations or simply: "I'm here." An acknowledgment that you showed up for another day.
- In a moment of stress when you feel you've messed up and the shame spiral starts, here's your 30-second ritual: Hand on heart. Three breaths. Say: "I'm a human who made a mistake. I'm still worthy of love." Then one action, apologise if needed, fix what you can, or simply move forward. The key is interrupting the hour-long self-attack with 30 seconds of self-loyalty.
- Try bathroom re-sets. You're already going to the bathroom multiple times a day. Make it a self-love checkpoint. After washing your hands, look at them. These hands that have comforted others, created things, held what you love. Say silently: "Thank you. I'm doing my best."

- Before Hard Conversations, create a one-minute boundary ritual: Both feet flat on floor. Hand on stomach. Three deep breaths into your belly. Say: "Whatever happens, I'm on my side. I won't abandon myself in this conversation." This pre-loads self-connection before you enter situations where you historically lose yourself.
- Before bed, instead of cataloguing failures, ask: "What's one moment today I chose myself?" Maybe you ate lunch sitting down. Maybe you said no to something. Maybe you cried instead of numbing. Find one moment, however small, put your hand over your heart and say "Thank you."
- Attach self-love to existing habits:
- Coffee brewing = hand on heart time
- Brushing teeth = mirror kindness
- Red lights = three breaths of self-approval
- Loading dishwasher = thanking your body

Emergency Protocols

Try this when self-hatred hits: you catch sight of yourself and feel disgust. You make a mistake and the inner critic goes nuclear. You compare yourself to someone and feel worthless. Here's your 60-second practice:

1. Name it: "I'm in self-attack mode"
2. Hands on body, press down firmly (grounding and holding yourself)
3. Say: "This is old programming talking. I don't have to believe it."

4. One kind act: drink water, step outside, text a friend

The goal is to interrupt the attack with one gesture of self-alliance.

You're on social media. Everyone's life looks better. You're failing at everything. STOP. Put the phone down. Both hands on heart. Say: "I'm comparing my insides to their outsides. My life is not meant to look like anyone else's." Then do something only you can do, call your grandmother, work on your weird project, dance to your favourite song.

If you're at work or in public and can't do anything too obvious, here's your stealth practice: Tap your thumb to each finger while internally saying: "I (tap) am (tap) choosing (tap) myself (tap)." Four words, four taps, two seconds. Repeat as needed.

For depression days, overwhelm seasons, or just life: Pick ONE thing. Maybe it's saying "good morning" to yourself. Maybe it's one conscious breath before sleep. Maybe it's touching your heart when you pass a mirror. One thing, done badly, counts.

When you realise you haven't practiced self-love in days/weeks/months, don't spiral. Use the return ritual: "Hello, I've been gone. I'm back now. We begin again." No punishment. No elaborate comeback. Just returning, which is its own radical act.

Feel free to pick and choose from these ideas. They're tiny rebellions against a lifetime of self-abandonment. They're promises to stop leaving yourself. They're practice for the revolutionary act of loving yourself.

Starting Where You Are

The truth about self-love is that it doesn't require you to feel loving. It requires small acts of loyalty to yourself, repeated until they become habit. Until choosing yourself becomes as natural as breathing.

Today, pick one transition in your day, maybe walking through your front door, and make it a moment of self-return. Touch the doorframe. Take one breath. Say internally "I'm choosing myself." That's it. That's the whole practice. Create a playlist that makes you feel good. Play it when you feel scattered. Let your body learn that these sounds mean safety, mean choosing connection over abandonment.

Some days the practice will feel natural. Other days, forced. Both are fine. The point is to keep showing up for yourself, one small gesture at a time, until self-love stops feeling like a practice and starts feeling like coming home.

Creating Your Morning Ritual: The First Spell of the Day

Dawn is when the veil is thinnest. In those blurry moments between sleep and waking, before your defences rebuild themselves, before the world rushes in with its urgent ordinary demands, you have a window. Not for manifestation or abundance or any of the glossy promises, but for the simplest, most radical magic of all: choosing yourself.

A morning ritual reverses this spell. It's not about becoming a morning person or achieving enlightenment before coffee. It's about creating a tiny sanctuary in time where you remember: I am not a problem to be solved. I am worthy of reverence.

Start here: before your eyes open, find your heartbeat. Just find it. Your hand knows the way. This beating is proof of your belonging here. No one's heart beats by accident. Say your own name, not how others say it when they're disappointed or rushed, but how you'd speak to someone you're impossibly glad to see.

The body holds magic if we let it. Stretch in bed, but stretch like you're remembering you have a body, like you're grateful for this soft animal that carried you through another night. When your feet first touch the floor, let them actually touch. The earth has been waiting all night to hold you up again.

Water is the first alchemy. When you wash your face, you're not just removing sleep. You're performing an ancient ritual of renewal. Every cupped handful of water is a chance to begin again. Pat your face dry like you're touching something precious, because you are.

The mirror is where most of us break the spell. We approach it like an enemy, scanning for flaws, building our case for unworthiness. What if you approached your reflection the way you'd approach a deer in the forest: gently, with wonder, without sudden movements? You don't have to love what you see. You just have to be willing to really see. To stay present with this human who's been through everything with you.

The kitchen holds its own power. When you make your coffee or tea, you're practicing transformation, beans into elixir, leaves into comfort. Stir clockwise to draw good things toward you. Hold the warm cup like you're receiving a gift, because you are: the gift of being able to give yourself what you need.

Your morning ritual doesn't need to look mystical to anyone else. It can be as simple as refusing to check your phone for ten minutes. As ordinary as making your bed while saying thank you to the night that held you. Consider choosing a few practices from the following list:

- Light a candle while coffee or tea brews
- Touch your heart before touching your phone
- Say your own name with tenderness
- Tape affirmations to your mirror and say them when you are getting ready
- Hold a meaningful object and connect in with love
- Play one song that means "I choose myself"
- Stretch like you're greeting your body
- Stand at window and bless the day
- Wash your face as sacred preparation for the day ahead
- Speak to your reflection with affirmations

- Say "Good morning" to yourself
- As you step from your bed, say "thank you"
- Appreciate something you like in your space such as a houseplant
- State your intentions for the day
- Blow a kiss to the mirror and receive it
- Thank your bed for holding you
- Sit with your journal while sipping tea, and write out affirmations
- Five minutes of gentle meditation to start the day (which could be a walking meditation or a reading meditation like the one near the end of this book)

4

MEETING THE SHADOW GENTLY

Sit quietly for a moment and let your attention drift inward. What parts of yourself do you keep hidden? What emotions do you swallow before they can be seen? What aspects of your personality have you locked away because someone, somewhere, told you they were unacceptable? Feel them stirring in the dark, not as monsters to be defeated, but as exiled children waiting to come home.

Clarissa Pinkola Estés speaks of La Loba, the wolf woman who must descend into the valley to sing flesh back onto the bones of the dead. The woman, who collects the old bones of wolves in the desert, ribs and vertebrae scattered by time and neglect. She gathers them tenderly, arranges them just so, and then she sings. And in her singing, what was dead returns to life.

This is shadow work. We are searching for our own scattered bones, the parts of ourselves we learned to bury, to reject, to pretend never existed. But unlike the stories that tell us to slay our dragons, this work asks us to sing them back to life.

Shadow work is like tending roses in winter - you must work with the thorns even when there are no blooms to reward you. But those thorns that draw blood are the same protection that allows the tender buds to survive. We cannot have the rose without accepting its fierce self-protection. We must face our own inner-protectors in order to make room for the live we want to grow into. Flowers, fruits and vegetables thrive on compost.

The most bountiful blooms and the sweetest fruits thrive on the decay of all the old crap that is no longer living. But it need to be let go of and broken down in order to become a rich source of nourishment. So too is shadow work, and the facing of what we have unconsciously cut off from ourselves, important in nourishing, healing and growing what we do want to see flourish in our inner world.

What Lives in Your Shadow

Carl Jung gave us the term "shadow" for the unconsicous and sometimes scary things that we try to escape hidden deep within us. Sometimes it appears most strongly at 3 AM when we're lying awake, remembering every cruel thing you've ever done. It's the flash of rage that surprises you, the neediness you despise in yourself, the ambition you've learned to hide. It's also, strangely enough, your joy that you felt you had to suppress, your delight that was too loud, your creativity that was too weird, your power that was too threatening.

The shadow is everything we've exiled to survive.

Across cultures and time, people have understood that trauma can cause parts of us to fragment or flee. This is echoed in the soul retrieval rituals of Siberia, Mongolia, the Americas, and Amazonian traditions, as well as in Celtic, Sumerian and Egyptian mythology. In Greek myth, Psyche is torn from Eros and must complete a series of soul-forging tasks to return to herself. In Celtic stories, the land falls barren when the king is wounded, showing how inner injury radiates outward until healing is sought. These myths speak to a deep truth echoed in modern psychotherapy "parts work": that within us live younger selves, exiled aspects, protectors and wounded inner children who split off to carry unbearable feelings. Healing doesn't mean erasing these parts, but meeting them with presence, listening to their stories, and inviting them back into wholeness. The moment a piece of the self departs to survive overwhelming pain. Each return is a reclamation and a building of who we are, more complete for having made the journey.

I began this work, consciously, in my early 20s, at the encouragement of Fiona, the Celtic shamanic practitioner who had been my counsellor when I was a teenager, but it was years before it became a more consious practice.

By July 2013 I was deep in my exploration of archetypes and I wrote: "The beginning of an archetypal journey can be quite muddled. You are scraping through the sediment of the conscious mind, digging deeper into the dark."

I saw myself in Clarissa's story of La Loba, the wolf woman, seeking her own wild nature through the bones in the dessert, stumbling in the darkness, looking for fragments of my own skeleton. Each therapy session, each journal entry, each moment of recognition was another bone collected. Peice by peice, I was bringing my whole self back together, slowly, consciously.

The Shadow as Sacred Protector

Every shadow quality is a protector in disguise. That harsh inner critic? She's trying to protect you from external criticism by getting there first. That buried rage? He's guarding your boundaries when you couldn't. That hidden neediness? She's preserving your capacity for connection, keeping it safe until someone worthy appears.

In 2013 I was writing about fairy tale archetypes when I realised the evil stepmother lived inside me too. "She is the inner voice of negative self-talk, the self-criticism, self-deprecation," I wrote. "She seeks to control the good and innocent elements of personality because she is afraid."

But afraid of what? When I got curious instead of combative, she revealed her terror: if I showed my true self, I'd be rejected, abandoned, annihilated. She'd been protecting me the only way she knew how, by making me small enough to be safe.

This is the powerful shift from seeing shadow as enemy to recognising shadow as guardian. Each exiled part has been holding something precious, keeping it safe in the only way it could.

Understanding Your Inner Parts

When we talk about shadow work, we're often wrestling with parts of ourselves that feel like enemies; the inner critic that won't shut up, the rage that terrifies us, the neediness we despise. But what if these shadow aspects aren't flaws to fix or demons to exorcise? Richard Schwartz's Internal Family Systems work reveals that each of us contains within us a vast collection of parts, many of them trying to protect us in their own way. These shadow parts aren't in the dark because they're bad; they're shadowy because we've banished them from the light of our awareness and in their unconsciousness they sometimes lash out like an upset child. When we turn toward them with curiosity instead of contempt, we discover that our shadows are full of protectors who've been working overtime, often since we were very young, trying to keep us safe the only way they know how.

Try this practice:

1. Choose a shadow quality you struggle with
2. Close your eyes and imagine this quality as a guardian
3. Ask with genuine curiosity: "What are you protecting me from?"
4. Listen not just with your mind but with your whole body

5. Thank this guardian for their service, even if their methods are outdated

When I did this with my inner critic, she showed me memories of childhood humiliation. She was still trying to protect that devastated child by ensuring I never stood out enough to be mocked again. Understanding her positive intention changed everything. I could work with her instead of against her.

The Intelligence of Exile

Every part of ourselves that lives in shadow was exiled for a reason. Usually, that reason was survival. The child who learns that anger means abandonment buries her fire so deep she forgets it exists. The teenager who discovers their sensitivity brings mockery builds walls so thick they can't feel their own heart. The adult who is afraid her authenticity threatens others can create such elaborate masks she forgets her own face.

This is the intelligence of the psyche doing whatever necessary to secure love, safety, belonging. Your shadow is proof of your resilience, evidence of how brilliantly you adapted to an environment that couldn't hold all of you.

The problem comes later, when the adaptation outlives its usefulness; When the anger you buried to keep your parents' love becomes an inability to set boundaries; When the sensitivity you hid to avoid mockery becomes an inability to feel joy; When the authenticity you masked to fit in becomes an existential emptiness you can't name.

The Anatomy of Shame

Beneath most shadow material lies shame, not just guilt that says "I did something wrong" but "I am something wrong." Shame is the guardian at the gate of the shadow realm, and until we learn to meet it with compassion, the deeper work remains inaccessible.

Shame has a distinct signature in the body:

- Heat rising to the face
- Chest collapsing inward
- Desire to hide or disappear
- Stomach dropping or churning
- Numbness or dissociation

Brené Brown's research reveals that shame thrives in silence, secrecy, and judgment. But it cannot survive empathy, compassion, and connection. This is why shadow work requires such gentleness, we're not just meeting rejected parts, we're meeting the shame that bound them. To free ourselves from shame, we require self-compassion.

When shame arises:

1. **Name it**: "I'm feeling shame right now"
2. **Locate it**: Where does it live in your body?
3. **Breathe into it**: Not to make it go away, but to be present
4. **Speak to it**: "Thank you for trying to protect me from rejection"

5. **Offer compassion**: Place your hand where you feel it and say, "It's safe to be human here"

Shadow work reveals we're all hiding the same human experiences. We can be gentle with ourselves and open up in self-compassion. This is the path to healing and we don't have to walk it all at once, but step-by-step, we can begin to free ourselves from the pain and shame that have been keeping us captive.

WHEN YOU LOOK at a newborn baby it's impossible to feel that they are worthy of shame, and yet we were all that tiny innocent creature once, before the world twisted us up into knots. Connect in with your own innocence with compassion for everything you've struggled with and suffered through. Accept it all. Forgive yourself. Set yourself free. This is your unique journey. Admire it for what it is, take a deep breath, and let go.

The Cultural Shadow

Your personal shadow doesn't exist in a vacuum. We inherit collective shadows, the rejected and shamed aspects of our cultures, communities, and ancestral lines. These cultural shadows become personal through internalization.

- Anger (labeled as bitchiness)
- Ambition (seen as threatening)
- Sexual desire (shamed as impure or dangerous)

- Power (condemned as manipulative)
- Vulnerability (mocked as weakness)
- Tenderness (rejected as unmanly)
- Need for connection (shamed as dependence)
- Artistic sensitivity (dismissed as impractical)

Layer onto this the shadows created by racism, classism, homophobia, and other systems of oppression, and we see how personal shadow work is always also political work. When you reclaim your right to feel anger, you're not just healing yourself, you're disrupting centuries of conditioning. When you embrace vulnerability, you're actually embracing a deeper strength.

Shadow work IS self-love work. Every time you turn toward a rejected part of yourself with curiosity instead of judgment, you're practicing self-love. Every shadow you integrate is a prodigal child welcomed home.

The Body Knows First

Before your mind recognises shadow material, your body knows. It knows in the way your throat closes when certain topics arise. It knows in the tension that grips your shoulders when you're asked about your dreams. It knows in the exhaustion that descends when you've been performing your acceptable self too long.

Shadow work is somatic work. The exiled parts of ourselves live in our tissues, our nervous system, our breath. You can't think your way to integration, you have to feel it.

For Repressed Anger:

- Make fists and gently pound a pillow while saying "I matter"
- Push against a wall with your full strength, feeling your power
- Growl, roar, or make primal sounds (in private or into a pillow)
- Vigorous movement: running, dancing, shaking
- Write an uncensored rage letter (then safely burn or bury it)

For Suppressed Grief:

- Place hands on your heart and rock gently
- Let yourself make whatever sounds want to come, moaning, keening, sighing
- Take a grief bath: warm water, low lights, permission to cry
- Movement: slow swaying, being held by gravity
- Create a grief altar with photos or objects of what's been lost

For Rejected Sensuality:

- Touch different textures mindfully
- Eat something delicious very slowly
- Take a luxurious bath or shower
- Wear clothes that feel good against your skin
- Dance in a way that feels sensual to you

When the Shadow Overwhelms

Sometimes shadow work feels less like gentle integration and more like being pulled under by a riptide. You start with good intentions, maybe you're journaling about old anger or sitting with grief you've avoided for years, and suddenly you're drowning. The feelings are too big, too fast, too much. Your body goes numb or won't stop shaking. Sleep becomes impossible, or when it comes, nightmares chase you back to waking. You find yourself reaching for whatever numbed you before, food, alcohol, scrolling, shopping, but now with the added shame of "failing" at healing.

This is when we need to recognise we're pushing too hard. We need to slow down or get help. Some shadows are simply too big to meet alone. Some wounds are so deep that trying to heal them without support can be like performing surgery on ourselves with no training.

Seeking professional help is an excellent idea, especially when trauma memories surface. A good trauma-informed therapist can be excellent inner medicine. There's no shame in needing this level of support. Shadow work isn't just a solo hero's journey; sometimes it's a team effort. Sometimes wisdom looks like admitting you've gone as far as you can go alone. Sometimes the bravest thing is picking up the phone and saying, "I need help holding this."

Integration as a Lifetime Practice

Shadow work is an ongoing relationship with the parts of yourself that live in darkness. Some days you'll feel like you're making progress. Other days you'll meet a piece of shadow so familiar you'll wonder if you've done any work at all. This is the path. We meet our shadows at deeper levels as we develop more capacity to hold them. In this work, our greatest wounds often hide our greatest gifts. The sensitivity that brought mockery becomes deep intuition. The anger that seemed dangerous becomes clear boundaries. The neediness that felt shameful becomes the capacity for deep intimacy.

As you work with the darker aspects of your shadow, you might notice something unexpected: glimpses of light you've also hidden away. Talents you minimised. Joy you dimmed. Power you pretended not to have. Meeting your shadow gently is perhaps the most courageous thing you'll ever do. It's also the deepest act of self-love, to turn toward what you've rejected and say, "You belong here too."

Your shadows are not your enemies. They're your protectors, your teachers, your hidden medicine. They've been holding your gifts in the dark, keeping them safe until you were ready. You don't have to meet every shadow today. You don't have to be fearless. You just have to be willing and curious instead of critical, willing to feel instead of fix, willing to welcome home what you've cast away.

The bones are scattered, yes. But you can gather them. You know the song, even if you've forgotten the words. And as you gather what's been lost, as you sing with whatever voice you have, you'll discover the magic: What you thought was dead within you was only sleeping. What you thought was monster was protector. What you thought was weakness was untapped power.

Breathe deep. The shadow is stirring, ready to teach you its wisdom. You are safe enough now to listen.

5

THE GOLDEN SHADOW & THE LIGHT YOU HID

Take a deep breath, put your hand over your heart and connect in. Now allow your mind to drift back and remember a moment when you felt utterly, radiantly alive. Maybe you were dancing with complete abandon. Maybe you were speaking passionately about something you loved. Maybe you were creating something beautiful, lost in the flow of your own brilliance. Feel that aliveness in your body, the expansion, the electricity, the uncontainable joy. Now notice: when did you learn to dim that light? Who taught you it wasn't safe to shine?

There's a particular cruelty in a world that teaches us to hide our light. We understand why we might feel pressured to bury our anger, our sadness, our neediness, but our brilliance? Our joy? Our natural magnificence? Yet these golden qualities often threaten others just as much as our darkness does, sometimes more.

Carl Jung observed this phenomenon, noting that we cast into shadow not only what seems negative but also what seems too positive, too bright, too much for our environment to hold.

Your golden shadow contains some of your most precious gifts: the confidence that others called "showing off," the sensitivity that was labelled "too much," the creativity that was deemed impractical, the leadership that was seen as threatening, the joy that made others uncomfortable.

The Conspiracy Against Brilliance

From the moment we begin to express our natural radiance, the world starts its work of dimming. Not from deliberate malice, usually, but from the discomfort our light creates in those who've learned to live in shadows.

Don't be too proud.

Stop showing off.

Calm down.

Don't get too excited.

Who do you think you are?

Don't be so sensitive.

That's not realistic.

These messages come from people who love us but who learned to dim their own light. They pass on their limitations not out of cruelty, but out of their own unhealed wounds. The parent who says "don't get your hopes up" is trying to protect you from the disappointment they've learned to expect. The teacher who says "stop being so dramatic" is uncomfortable with the bigness of emotion they've learned to suppress.

Tall Poppy Syndrome

In many cultures, there's an unspoken rule that no one should stand out too much, shine too brightly, or claim their power too boldly. The tall poppy gets cut down. The nail that sticks up gets hammered. We learn that visibility equals danger, that excellence invites attack, that being special makes you a target.

For women especially, this conditioning runs deep. Be smart, but not intimidating. Be beautiful, but not vain. Be successful, but not ambitious. Be creative, but not impractical. The golden shadow for women often holds leadership, sexual power, intellectual brilliance, and unapologetic self-expression.

For men, different aspects get shadowed: artistic sensitivity gets buried as "unmanly," emotional intelligence is hidden as "soft," the desire for beauty and tenderness gets locked away. The golden shadow holds the poet, the dancer, the gentle father, the vulnerable human.

In collectivist cultures, individual brilliance might be seen as threatening group harmony. The golden shadow holds personal ambition, unique expression, standing out. In individualist cultures, while celebrating individual success, there's often shame around needing others, collaborative gifts, or communal joy. In some communities, intelligence might be shadowed as "getting above yourself," while artistic pursuits could be seen as impractical luxuries. At times, authentic expression, flamboyance, and brilliance often gets pushed into shadow for safety.

Impostor Syndrome

Almost everyone has experienced some kind of impostor syndrome. Before we can reclaim our golden shadow, we often must face the fear: "They're going to find out you don't belong here. You're not as smart/talented/qualified as they think."

Surprisingly, impostor syndrome is actually evidence of your golden shadow. People usually feel like a fraud in areas where they have real gifts. It's less common to get impostor syndrome about things they can't do at all. The intensity of the impostor feeling often correlates directly with the power of the hidden gift, the suppressed brilliance that is shining through the darkness, hoping to be unearthed.

When I first started sharing my writing publicly, the impostor syndrome was overwhelming. "Who am I to think I have anything worth saying?" But that very intensity was my psyche recognising how much writing mattered to me, how central it was to my authentic expression.

Instead of fighting impostor syndrome, try this:

1. **Thank it**: "Thank you for showing me where my gifts live"
2. **Get specific**: What exact gift is it guarding? Leadership? Creativity? Intelligence?
3. **Find the origin**: When did you first learn this gift was dangerous to express?
4. **Dialogue with it**: "I know you're trying to keep me safe from criticism/rejection. What if we tried visibility in small doses?"
5. **Evidence gathering**: Keep a file of positive feedback to read when impostor syndrome strikes

The fact that you feel like an impostor means you're stretching into your growth edge. It's evidence of expansion, not fraud.

How We Hide Our Light in Daily Life

The golden shadow reveals itself through the opportunities we mysteriously sidestep. That promotion you don't apply for, telling yourself you need just one more qualification. The manuscript that lives on your hard drive because it's "not quite ready" after five years of revisions. The way your voice goes up at the end of sentences when you know exactly what you're talking about, turning statements into questions, expertise into uncertainty.

We undercharge for our services and feel guilty when clients happily pay. We sit in meetings while someone else pitches the idea we mentioned at the coffee machine last week. We call our art a hobby, our writing a distraction, our music something we "mess around with", anything to avoid claiming the identity of creator. There's always someone more qualified, more talented, more deserving of recognition. Anyone but us.

In relationships, the dimming becomes almost automatic. We choose partners who need us small so they can feel secure. We perform less intelligence than we possess, less knowing, less power. When friends struggle with our successes, we learn to hide them, to downplay achievements, to make ourselves digestible. We apologise for our intuitions, our emotions, our insights, as if seeing clearly is something to be sorry for.

Money becomes another place we play small. Success arrives and we sabotage it, unconsciously proving we don't deserve abundance. We give away our work because charging feels "greedy," not recognising that undervaluing ourselves teaches others to undervalue us too. We stay in jobs that use maybe a third of our gifts, telling ourselves we're lucky to have work at all. The golden shadow convinces us that wanting more, more recognition, more money, more creative expression, is selfish, when really it's just human.

My Journey with the Hidden Light

In my journey towards becoming a professional writer, I had to push through many walls of shame and impostor syndrome. I felt insecure and anxious about creative exposure, fear of death through vulnerability. I was terrified of character assassination and being "cancelled" no matter how careful I was. The printed word is unforgiving. It remembers. I have no doubt that some common words I use now will be inappropriate in ten years, and yet I pushed through this terror because staying small and hidden was a far worse fate for me.

Just as Anaïs Nin wrote: "And the day came when the risk to remain tight in a bud was more painful than the risk it took to blossom." My fear and the impostor syndrome I faced were evidence of how deeply my creativity mattered to me, how much I longed to share my gifts with the world. But somewhere along the way, I'd learned that creative exposure was dangerous. That being seen in my full expression might lead to annihilation.

The affirmations I created were acts of reclamation:

- "I feel proud of my novels and other creative writing"
- "I have valuable things to say and my creativity helps me to share understanding with a wide audience"
- "I am strong enough to stand in my vulnerability"
- "I understand that people project all kinds of things into what they read and I only take on-board what is useful for me"

Each affirmation was permission to shine, to be visible, to take up space with my gifts. But oh, how my body resisted at first. My throat would close. My hands would shake. My inner critic would scream, "Who do you think you are?"

This is the psyche trying to keep us safe within familiar bounds. If joy was dangerous in childhood, too much joy now triggers old alarms. If success meant abandonment, success now feels threatening.

Jealousy as a Golden Shadow Teacher

One of the most reliable maps to our golden shadow is jealousy. Not the mild "I wish I had that" feeling, but the burning, uncomfortable envy that makes us want to look away. That intensity is recognition, your soul seeing its own unexpressed potential in another. Try this:

1. **List everyone you're jealous of** (be ruthlessly honest)
2. **Get specific**: What exact quality or achievement triggers you?
3. **Feel the feeling**: Where does jealousy live in your body?
4. **Translate it**: "I'm jealous of her confidence" becomes "I have hidden confidence"
5. **Find the fear**: What am I afraid would happen if I expressed this quality?
6. **Take one tiny action**: Express 1% of that quality today

The alchemy happens when we can say: "Thank you for showing me what's possible. Thank you for modelling what I'm capable of." The person you're jealous of becomes a guide, showing you your own hidden territory.

But this only works with genuine integration. Spiritual bypassing would say "I'm not jealous, I'm inspired!" True shadow work says "I'm jealous AND I can learn from this. My jealousy is showing me my own light."

The Shadow of Success and Abundance

We say we want success, but watch how quickly we backpedal when it arrives. The fear lives deeper than logic, in our bones, in our ancestry, in every story we absorbed about what happens to people who rise. Maybe you're afraid of outgrowing your family, becoming unrecognizable to the people who loved you when you were struggling. Or success means visibility, and visibility means being a target for envy, criticism, attack.

For some of us, the identity of seeker, of struggler, has become so familiar we don't know who we'd be without it. What if we achieve everything we said we wanted and still feel empty? What if success doesn't equal happiness? What if becoming successful means becoming someone we don't like, a sellout, inauthentic, just another person who chose money over meaning?

Financial abundance carries particularly deep shadows. Women inherit centuries of not being allowed to own property or earn money, our bodies remember that financial power was dangerous, forbidden, unwomanly. If you come from poverty, success can feel like betrayal, like you're abandoning everyone still struggling, leaving your people behind. Spiritual seekers wrestle with the poisonous myth that money is evil, that caring about abundance means you're not evolved. Artists inherit the story of the starving artist, as if suffering creates better art, as if comfort kills creativity.

When money starts flowing toward you, notice your body's response. The nausea, the anxiety, the urge to give it all away or spend it quickly so you can return to familiar scarcity. Your nervous system might be rejecting abundance because somewhere you learned that financial success means selling out, being greedy, forgetting where you came from.

Healing the Abundance Shadow

Start by examining your inheritance. What stories about money did you absorb from your family? Write them down, all of them, the spoken and unspoken rules about who deserves wealth, what money does to people, why your people don't have it. Write a letter to money as if it were a person. What would you say? What resentments would pour out? What fears? What desires you've never admitted?

Practice receiving in small ways before you tackle the big ones. When someone compliments you, don't deflect. Say thank you. Let it land. When help is offered, accept it without immediately offering something in return. Notice how uncomfortable this makes you. That discomfort is your golden shadow speaking.

Set prices that reflect your worth, not your fear. Start tracking evidence that money can be used for good, that abundance doesn't corrupt everyone, that you can have financial success without becoming someone you hate. Celebrate others' abundance without making it mean something about your lack. Their success doesn't steal yours. There's enough for everyone, but first you have to believe you're included in "everyone."

The Body Language of Dimming

Your body has become expert at making you smaller. It happens so fast you don't even notice, someone compliments your intelligence and you physically shrink, shoulders rounding, voice getting quieter. You've learned a whole choreography of diminishment. The way you add "just" to everything: "I just thought..." "It's just an idea..." "I'm just lucky..." The way you turn statements into questions, your voice lilting up at the end, asking permission to know what you know.

Watch what happens when someone praises your work. Do you immediately point out its flaws? Change the subject? Redirect the compliment back to them? These micro-movements of deflection are your golden shadow in action, protecting you from the danger of being seen as valuable. Your body remembers every time visibility brought pain, and it's still trying to keep you safe the only way it knows how.

Embodied Practices for Reclaiming Your Light

Different shadows need different medicine. If leadership is your golden shadow, practice taking up space. Stand in power postures, yes, like Wonder Woman, feet wide, hands on hips, chin up. It feels ridiculous until it doesn't. Speak from your belly instead of your throat; let your voice carry weight. Practice holding eye contact, first with yourself in the mirror, then with others. Enter rooms like you belong there, sit with expansive posture instead of making yourself compact.

For suppressed creativity, the medicine is unstructured expression. Dance with your eyes closed to music without words. Scribble without trying to draw anything. Hum or tone without turning it into a song. Work with clay just to feel it move through your fingers. Creation is your birthright.

If intelligence is what you've hidden, practice speaking your thoughts aloud with conviction. Share one insight daily without prefacing it with apologies. Write stream of consciousness about what you know, not what you've learned from others, but what you understand in your bones. Teach something to an imaginary audience, letting yourself be the expert you actually are.

For beauty or sensuality shadows, the practice is presence with your own form. Look at yourself with soft eyes, increasing the time you can hold your own gaze without criticism. Dress with intention, not for others but for the pleasure of adorning yourself. Engage each sense deliberately throughout the day. Dance, focusing on how movement feels in your body, not how it looks from outside.

Permission Slips for Radiance

Sometimes the psyche needs explicit permission to reclaim what it's hidden. Write yourself formal authorization to shine. Make it specific: "I give myself permission to be intelligent without apology." "I give myself permission to succeed beyond my family's comfort zone." "I give myself permission to be joyful even when others are struggling." "I give myself permission to charge what I'm worth." "I give myself permission to outgrow anyone who needs me to stay small."

Post these permissions where you'll see them. Say them aloud to your reflection. Your nervous system needs time to adjust to the possibility that magnificence might be safe. That you can be powerful without being perfect. That your light doesn't steal anyone else's, there's enough brightness for everyone.

When Others React to Your Light

As you reclaim your golden shadow, your relationships will reorganise. Some people will celebrate your emergence like they've been waiting for it all along. Others will feel threatened, like your brightness is a personal attack on their choice to stay dim. This sorting process is painful but necessary. You'll learn who was invested in your smallness, who needs you diminished to feel secure, who can grow alongside you, and who has their own golden shadow work to do.

For relationships you want to preserve, be patient but not self-betraying. Share your journey without trying to convince anyone to join you. Give people time to adjust to your changes. Model what's possible without preaching. But don't dim yourself to make others comfortable. Sometimes love means letting go of people who need you to stay small. This is heartbreaking shadow work, grieving relationships that required your self-abandonment.

The Spiritual Bypass Warning

Reclaiming your golden shadow isn't about toxic positivity or spiritual bypassing. It's not about denying problems exist or floating above human struggles on a cloud of "love and light." True golden shadow work means shining while honouring others' pain, being brilliant and humble, expressing joy while holding space for grief, claiming your gifts while continuing to grow.

Watch for spiritual ego, using your light as a new way to feel superior. When you catch yourself thinking you're more evolved than others because you've reclaimed some brilliance, return to basics: "I approve of myself. I am human. I am learning." Being magnificent doesn't mean being better than anyone. It means being fully yourself, which includes your flaws, your struggles, your thoroughly human heart.

Living with Reclaimed Light

Reclaiming your golden shadow is an ongoing journey. Life will test your commitment to visibility. Loss might make joy feel inappropriate. Failure might make you question your gifts. Criticism might reactivate old wounds. Success might trigger upper limit problems, that moment when things are going too well and you unconsciously sabotage to return to familiar struggle.

The path of this journey to knowing and loving yourself deeply winds in spirals, in and out, which means you'll meet these shadows at different depths throughout life. The creative confidence you reclaim at thirty might need different medicine at fifty. This is the natural deepening of self-acceptance. Each time you choose visibility over hiding, each time you let yourself shine despite the fear, you strengthen your capacity to hold your own light.

Create a golden shadow altar if it helps, a space dedicated to your brilliance. Include symbols of your hidden gifts, photos of yourself genuinely shining, gold candles for your inner radiance, mirrors for practicing seeing your own light. Add your written permissions, evidence of your gifts, fresh flowers for your continuous blooming. Visit this altar when dimming feels easier than shining. Let it remind you that your light is necessary. The world needs what you've been hiding. Your brilliance isn't selfish; it's service. But first, you have to be willing to let yourself shine.

The Truth About Your Hidden Light

You're not trying to become brilliant. You already are. The light isn't something you need to create or earn or prove, it's what you've been carefully hiding, probably since you were very young. It's still there, waiting under all the apologies and qualifications and "I'm not really that good at this" disclaimers.

Think about who you were before you learned to dim yourself. That child who danced without wondering if they looked stupid, who created art without calling it amateur, who led games on the playground without questioning their right to have ideas. That version of you didn't disappear. They went underground, but they're still there in your cells, in your impulses, in the things you do when you forget to monitor yourself.

Your golden shadow isn't some ideal future self you need to transform into. It's the parts of you that were always there until someone or something convinced you they were dangerous. The sensitivity you learned to call weakness. The intelligence you learned to downplay. The creativity you learned to hide. The leadership you learned to soften. These aren't new qualities to develop, they're your birthright qualities to reclaim.

Reclaiming your light doesn't mean you float above human struggle on some enlightened cloud. You can be brilliant and still struggle with depression. You can recognise your gifts and still wrestle with your shadows. You can shine while grieving, succeed while healing, be magnificent while asking for help. Integration means accepting the full spectrum, your darkness and your light both get to exist, both get to be real, both get to matter.

The world needs what you've been hiding, but not because you should sacrifice yourself on the altar of service. It needs your particular way of seeing, your specific combination of gifts, your exact frequency of brilliance. When you create from joy instead of duty, it carries different medicine. When you lead from wholeness instead of proving, it opens different doors. When you shine without apology, you become permission for others to do the same.

Every time you charge what you're worth, you challenge systems that profit from undervaluing us. Every time you share your real work instead of your safe work, you expand what's possible. Every time you refuse to make yourself smaller to help someone else feel bigger, you disrupt patterns that have kept too many of us in hiding.

Those voices that told you to dim it down, tone it down, calm it down, they were wrong. Not evil, necessarily. Probably scared. Definitely limited. But wrong about you, wrong about what's too much, wrong about what the world needs. You aren't too bright or too powerful or too creative or too sensitive. You're exactly as much as you're meant to be. The world has been waiting for your full wattage, not some dimmer-switch version you think might be more palatable.

So maybe it's time to stop apologising for your radiance. Stop pretending you don't know what you know. Stop acting like your gifts are accidents instead of medicine.

Not because you owe it to anyone else, but because hiding is exhausting and you've been tired for so long. Because your light, unedited and unapologetic, is your truth. And living in truth, even when it scares you, is the only way to really live.

Stand up. Spread your arms wide. Take up all the space you need. Feel your light radiating from every cell. This is who you are when you stop hiding. This is your golden shadow coming home. This is you, approved of, devoted to, integrated, and finally free to shine.

6

THE BODY AS TEMPLE, NOT PROJECT

Place your hand on your belly. Feel it rise and fall with your breath. This simple touch, skin meeting skin, warmth recognising warmth, might be the first time today you've acknowledged this faithful vessel. Notice what arises: tenderness? Criticism? Numbness? Disconnection? Whatever you feel, know this: your body has been waiting for you. Patiently. Faithfully. Like a devoted friend who never stops hoping you'll return.

We live in exile from our own self. This is the lived reality of existing in a culture that teaches us to see our bodies as problems to solve, projects to perfect, inconveniences to override. We learn early that bodies are shameful, unruly, never quite right. Too big, too small, too loud, too needy, too much, not enough.

But what if everything we've been taught about bodies is a lie designed to keep us disconnected from our deepest source of wisdom, power, and presence?

We are born as sensing, reaching, wailing, suckling, wriggling creatures. And then, over time, we are taught to retreat. To be quiet. To be still. To be small. To override the messages of our body. To diet when we are hungry. To push through when we are tired. To smile when we feel rage.

In this culture, the body becomes a site of control, not celebration. We are taught to see it as a project. Something to fix, discipline, perfect. But the body never asked for perfection. It asked to be heard.

Body image is not simply about how we look , it is about how we relate to our own aliveness. When that relationship is severed, we live in tension. But when we reconnect, the tension begins to melt.

In *The Body is Not an Apology*, Sonya Renee Taylor writes, "We cannot build a movement for justice and liberation on a foundation of self-hate." She reminds us that radical self-love , and radical embodied love , are revolutionary acts. The body, returned to itself, becomes a source of truth. A compass. A sanctuary.

Our bodies, like rose bushes, have their seasons. They bloom and rest, expand and contract. A rose doesn't apologise for its dormant season or feel shame about its thorns. It lives its cycles, trusting that what appears dead in winter holds tomorrow's blooms.

The Great Disconnection

The exile from our bodies often happens slowly, through ten thousand small betrayals. Some people even learn to leave their body, to disassociate in order to protect. Some of us live from the neck up, treating the body like an unfortunate vehicle we are forced to drag around.

Many of us experience disconnection from our bodies, even if we've had relatively peaceful childhoods. We all experience powerlessness that drives us towards escape, to freeze and shut down, to fight our way towards safety or flight (run away), or to fawn (another lesser known survival response where we deliberately please other people to try to make the situation safer or easier and try to get safety through appeasing others).

When you can't escape, dissociation is intelligence, when your body is the site of shame or trauma, leaving it is survival. But what serves us in one season can imprison us in another. The protective mechanism becomes the cage. Sometimes the disconnection is much more subtle – we simply feel tired, exhausted. We'd rather escape into scrolling or streaming shows or eating for comfort.

Resmaa Menakem points out that "Trauma is not a flaw or weakness. It is a highly effective tool of safety and survival." Every way you've learned to leave your body was brilliant at the time. Dissociation protected you when staying present was unbearable. Hypervigilance kept you safe in unpredictable environments. Numbing helped you survive overwhelming sensations. The tension in your shoulders, the clenching in your jaw, these aren't failures. They're the physical evidence of your intelligence, the ways your body learned to protect you.

The goal isn't to eliminate these responses, it's to honour them, understand them, and slowly teach your body that what was once necessary for survival may not be needed now. But slowly. So slowly. At the pace of trust, not the pace of urgency.

Before we dive into practices of return, it's important to think about the ideal window for growth and healing, not stretching too far into extremes. Deb Dana, who translates polyvagal theory into practical application, teaches about the "window of tolerance", the zone where we can experience activation without becoming overwhelmed. This concept can help us understand why some body practices felt healing while others felt retraumatising.

Within our window, we can feel sensations without going into panic, experience emotions without drowning in overwhelm, and stay present. Outside our window, we're either in hyperarousal, heart racing, panic rising, the feeling that we might die, or hypoarousal, numb, floating, gone. Neither state allows for integration or healing.

Hillary McBride, in her book The Wisdom of Your Body, emphasises: "We cannot heal what we cannot feel, but we also cannot feel what doesn't feel safe to feel." In your daily life, when you feel yourself going into overwhelm or shutting down in numbness, take a moment, even if it's just excusing yourself to go to the bathroom.

It takes about twenty minutes to fully calm down from these states, and you might not have twenty minutes spare at that very moment, but give yourself whatever space you can. Hold yourself by putting your hand over your heart or belly, or wrapping your arms around yourself, stroking your own arms, gently.

Exhale slowly. Pause. Inhale slowly and deeply. Pause.

Good. You're doing well. Let yourself know it. Say the affirmations that feel grounding. I accept myself. I approve of myself. I am enough. I love myself, whichever ones feel easeful and centring. If you can, go for a walk and let each step ground you further into your being, into your presence. You are stronger here. Your mind is clearer. You are in a much better situation to make decisions and far, far more productive than when you're stressed and frantic. Rest can be the best productivity, so be gentle with yourself and prioritise coming back to presence.

The journey back to the body can require titration, a term from chemistry meaning to add something drop by drop until you reach the desired result. We return to our bodies drop by drop, at the pace of safety, not the pace of urgency.

Start with external sensation before diving into internal awareness. Feel the texture of your clothes. Notice temperature on your skin. Listen to sounds around you. Let your nervous system remember: sensation can be neutral, even pleasant.

Use movement to discharge old energy. Trauma specialist Bessel van der Kolk notes that trauma gets stuck in the body and needs to move. Gentle shaking, like animals do after threat. Walking while feeling your feet meet earth. Dancing to one song, letting your body lead. These practices help old energy complete its cycle and release.

Stay in choice. The moment body practices feel mandatory, they become another way we override ourselves. Build a healthy relationship with your body, gently, one breath at a time. You are choosing this, you are choosing you.

Navigating the Minefield of Diet Culture

We need to talk about food and weight, about the wellness industry that often masks diet culture as "health." Christy Harrison, in "Anti-Diet," writes: "Wellness culture is diet culture in a sneaky disguise." This disguise makes it even more insidious, wrapping restriction in the language of self-care.

Many of us spend years worrying about healthy eating. But underneath is the same old song: "My body is wrong and needs fixing". Every "wellness protocol" can be another way to override the body's actual signals. The path back to body wisdom around food is treacherous when you've spent years, maybe decades, fighting hunger, overriding fullness, categorising foods as good or evil. How do you trust a body whose signals you've systematically suppressed?

You start where you are. Maybe you begin by simply noticing hunger and fullness without acting on it, just gathering data about sensations you've learned to ignore.

Maybe you practice eating without screens, tasting food you usually inhale while distracted. Maybe you notice the voices that arise when you eat something previously forbidden, and you get curious about whose voices those are. The more we connect in, the easier it is for our body to communicate with us about what it's really craving, not just filling the void of emotional eating, but the rich nutrition that we are seeking out at a deeper level.

Ignore what diet experts tell you and listen to your own body. We are all different. How do you feel after eating one kind of breakfast, compared to another? Does a high protein lunch give you energy to override the afternoon slump? Do carbohydrates make you sleepy, and if so, are they better to save for dinner time?

Eating to fill an emotional void creates extra work for our digestive systems and can further disconnect us from our bodies. And besides, it's not very good for resolving emotions unless we can get our emotions onboard. At times, that tub of ice cream can be exactly what you need, but if you're feeling guilty, bad or wrong about the choice you're only adding to your problems. Instead, let yourself off the hook. Notice those guilty tapes playing in your mind and forgive yourself, set yourself free. Enjoy that ice cream! Enjoy it with such easefulness, bliss and wild abandon that it's actually really good for you. Create a powerful peak experience out of your comfort food so that it's actually doing you good. In a restful embodied state, our bodies digest better, and we feel better which enables us to then make good choices about what we do next.

Reclaiming the Erotic as Life Force

In my early life, I, like many of us, absorbed shame about sexuality from family, school, the media. On a deep inner level, something about sexuality felt unsafe, and yet I wanted to experience all the joys and pleasures of human existance in a healthy and powerful way. I spent years trying to untangle this. For the longest time, I could only connect with my sexuality in my own private way, or in the throes of early infatuation. I felt blocked. I realised I had deep-seated fear, disconnecting me from my own body.

We cannot talk about embodiment without addressing sexuality and the erotic. In her book on reconnecting with our bodies and desire, Come As You Are, Emily Nagoski shares the insight that "We thrive when we have a positive goal to move toward, not just a negative state we're trying to move away from." Yet many of us carry trauma, shame, or disconnection that makes embodiment feel dangerous specifically in this realm.

The erotic is not just about sex, as Audre Lorde teaches. It's about being in touch with our deepest life force, our capacity for joy, our power to feel. It's the full-bodied YES to existence. But when sexuality has been a site of shame, trauma, or disconnection, accessing this life force feels impossible or terrifying.

Can you feel pleasure in the taste of chocolate melting on your tongue? In sunlight on your skin? In the perfect temperature of bath water? These are all erotic experiences, experiences of the body saying yes to sensation, to aliveness, to pleasure as birthright.

Kasia Urbaniak, author of the powerful book, Unbound, spent years in both Taoist monasteries and New York dungeons, learning about pleasure and power: "Life force has a distinctly erotic quality." It's that hum of aliveness that runs through everything when we're truly present, the same current that makes food taste better when you're actually hungry, that makes music sound different when you let it move through your whole body, that makes touch electric when you're fully there to receive it.

But we've been trained to compress ourselves. To make ourselves smaller, quieter, less needy, less wanting. We've learned to follow rules that no longer serve us - maybe never did - because following them supposedly makes us "good." In that tension and pressure to be good we're cut off from our life force, walking around half-dead and calling it virtue. Many of us spend years trying to be the good child, the good student, the good friend, the good worker, the good parent. Never too much, never too needy. Always checking if we are acceptable. And you know what? In that contracted state, we can't access our full power.

When we're disconnected from our life force, we literally can't tell the difference between selfish and generous. We give from emptiness and wonder why we're resentful. We deny our desires and wonder why we feel dead inside. But when we're actually embodied, actually feeling that current of aliveness, something miraculous happens. We know when we're full. We know when our giving comes from overflow rather than depletion. We know when our yes is real and when it's just fear dressed up as politeness.

Over the years, I've opened up more and more to my own experience of pleasure and desire. Even now, I'm still learning how to connect. After so much time, I've found a partner who understands me at my deepest levels, who is teaching me about the magic of the sensual.It's never too late, but opening up to new experiences involves surrender to vulnerability. Trust can be terrifying.

Your body knows things your mind has been trained to ignore. Your desires aren't character flaws. Your life force is the compass pointing you toward what's real, what's vital, what's actually yours to live. And that aliveness? It doesn't make you selfish. It makes you real.

The Aging Body in an Anti-Aging World

In a culture that sees aging as failure, how do we love bodies that are changing, softening, slowing? Every grey hair is treated as betrayal. Every wrinkle as defeat. Every slowing down as something to fight against rather than honour. I was lucky to be raised by a mother who refused to be self-tormented about grey hairs and wrinkles and instead claimed them as signs of wisdom.

I watch my body changing, the lines deepening around my eyes, the softening of what was once firm, the new aches that greet me in the morning. Ursula K. Le Guin wrote: "I am sick of the spiritual blindness of my culture that makes us fear aging and death rather than honour it." To age is to have survived. To age is to carry stories in our cells. To age is to embody time itself. We can learn to greet our aging bodies with curiosity rather than dread. To thank what's leaving, the effortless energy of youth, and welcome what's arriving, the wisdom that comes from having weathered seasons.

To reclaim the body is a returning to what you can actually feel, the ache in your hips, the warmth in your hands, the way breath moves through you without your permission or control. Most of us live so far from our own sensation that we don't even realise we've left.

Start with something almost insultingly simple. Bring your hand to your chest. Feel the rise and fall, not the idea of breathing but the actual movement under your palm. Let your hand become heavy there. Notice the texture of your own skin, the temperature, the rhythm that continues whether you pay attention or not. Let yourself know: "I am here," because speaking to yourself with kindness might be the most radical thing you do today.

Press your feet into the floor. Actually press them. The ground has been waiting to hold you this whole time, but you have to let it. You have to feel the connection instead of floating somewhere above your life, managing your body like a reluctant employee instead of living inside it.

The nervous system thrives on rhythm, breath, heartbeat, footsteps, the sway of walking. When you create consistent patterns of care, your body starts to believe you might not abandon it again. That trust becomes the foundation for everything else. Without it, all the shadow work and golden shadow reclamation stays theoretical, trapped in your head while your body continues its vigilant watch for danger.

When you are feeling courageous, look yourself in the eye in the mirror. Let your gaze soften. Look at your face as a story rather than an image. Every line was earned. Every shadow has a history. The curve of your mouth knows things about joy and sorrow that no one else will ever fully understand.

Speak to what you see, but speak gently: "I see how tired you are. I see how you've tried. I honour what you've carried. I'm here with you now." Move your gaze slowly down your body, not scanning for problems but acknowledging what's there. When feelings of "not enough" or shame rise, breathe with the emotions. When grief comes stay present. You don't have to change the feeling, just meet it without running.

Words combined with touch can reach the parts of us that went into hiding. Place your hand on any part of your body that feels numb, criticised, or abandoned. The belly you've hated. The thighs you've hidden. The scars you've covered. Speak directly to these places: "You are allowed. You are safe. You belong here. You are part of me."

Say it slowly, like drops of water on dry earth. This is reparenting your body, offering the acceptance that was withheld, the safety that was missing, the belonging you've been seeking everywhere but here.

When Your Body Feels Like the Enemy

Here's what many self-help teachings skip: what do you do when your body is a site of chronic pain, illness, or disability? How do you "come home" to a body that feels like it's betraying you?

I, myself, struggled with chronic pain, chronic fatigue syndrome, anxiety and depression since I was twelve years old. The self-work I've done has made a huge impact on these things for me, but not by bypassing them, by releasing old pain stored in the body, by being gentle with myself, by finding better ways to rest and look after myself, and by telling soothing, healing stories. Plenty of research shows that stress is terrible for the body, exacerbating health problems.

Sometimes the stories we tell ourselves about our bodies can literally make us sicker. I'm not saying your pain isn't real - it absolutely is. But research shows that our expectations about pain, illness, and healing have profound physical effects that go far beyond "it's all in your head."

Scientists call it the nocebo effect - when negative expectations create actual physical harm. In one study, a woman was warned that acupuncture might cause "cardiovascular collapse" in rare cases. She immediately suffered one, her heart rate dropping to 23 beats per minute. She had to be revived with a drip. The expectation alone nearly killed her.

Around 70-80% of research participants experience medicine symptoms that doctors tell them about even if they are given sugar pills rather than the medicine. This knowledge has led to new training for doctors in how to carefully communicate about medicine without causing more health problems!

When you live with chronic pain or illness, you naturally become hypervigilant about your body. Every twinge becomes a threat. Every bad day feels like proof that you're getting worse. And here's the devastating part: that vigilance, that expectation of pain, can actually amplify your symptoms. Studies show that simply warning patients "this may hurt" before a blood draw makes the pain more likely and more intense.

But our brains can create additional suffering through negative expectations, they can also create relief through different stories. Not the toxic positivity kind that says "just think happy thoughts and your illness will disappear." That's cruel and wrong. I'm talking about something gentler and more honest.

What if, instead of bracing for pain every morning, you approached your body with curiosity? "I wonder how we'll feel today?" What if, instead of "my body is broken," you tried "my body is doing its best with a difficult situation"? These aren't magic words that cure chronic illness. They're small shifts that can alleviate the suffering that our fearful and heavy thoughts might bring.

In my own journey with chronic pain and fatigue, I've learned that the stories I tell matter. When I say "I'm having a flare-up," my body seems to brace for the worst. But when I say "my body is asking for extra care today," something softens. The pain might still be there, but I'm not adding fear on top of it.

The research shows that simple rituals of wellness can help, even if they are entirely made up. The research on open-label placebos is particularly fascinating for those of us with chronic conditions. People taking sugar pills *while knowing they were sugar pills* still experienced significant symptom improvement in conditions like IBS, chronic back pain, and fatigue. About 70% of IBS patients improved just from taking pills they knew were placebos. Their bodies responded to the ritual of care, the act of doing something healing, even without active medication.

This doesn't mean you should stop your treatments or that your condition isn't real. It means that alongside whatever medical care you're receiving, you can work with your mind's powerful influence on your body. You can choose stories that soothe rather than scare. You can create rituals of care that signal safety to your nervous system. Every little blessing can help:

I'm doing my best. Today I will be gentle with myself. I accept myself. I have compassion for my body. I am open to healing. I choose easeful thoughts. I open to rejuvenation.

Some days will still be hard. Some days the pain will win. But knowing about nocebo effects gives us one more tool: the power to stop accidentally making things worse with our fears. Your body isn't your enemy. Your body is a beautiful frightened animal that needs gentle reassurance. And sometimes, changing the story we tell is the beginning of changing the experience itself.

The inner work we do have power over really can help, but there are pitfalls here. It's easy for people to feel that "not doing the work" is yet another failing to add to their list of things wrong with them, or to feel guilty.

I've watched friends navigate this territory, the friend with fibromyalgia who wakes to pain every morning, the friend whose chronic illness means some days she can barely lift her head, the friend whose autoimmune disease turned her body into a battlefield. For them, "just feel your feelings" or "trust your body" can feel like mockery.

Sonya Renee Taylor offers this wisdom: "We do not have to love our bodily difference or the experience of oppression in our bodies, we just have to love ourselves in our bodies." This distinction matters. You don't have to love pain. You don't have to be grateful for illness. But you can learn to have a better relationship with it, to feel empowered and tell more optimistic stories, to embrace small moments of joy, and to be present with yourself through it.

My friend Helena suffers from chronic pain and developed what she calls "micro-moments of pleasure." She can't feel good in her whole body, so she finds one square inch that feels neutral or pleasant, maybe the inside of her wrist, maybe her earlobe. She focuses there, building a tiny sanctuary of sensation that isn't pain. From that sanctuary, compassion can grow.

Grieving openly can also be a powerful release for old emotions so that they can release, leaving more space for lightness and new hope. Helena freed herself from limiting mental blocks around her chronic illness by creating grief rituals for the healthy body she'd wanted to have. She wrote letters to her pre-illness self, held ceremonies for lost abilities, cried for the future she'd imagined. "I had to mourn the healthy body," she told me, "before I could even begin to accept this one." As Roxane Gay writes, "This is my body, and I am learning to live in it. I am learning to love it, no matter how difficult that may be."

The groundbreaking ACE (Adverse Childhood Experiences) study revealed how childhood trauma, from abuse and neglect to household dysfunction, literally reshapes our bodies and brains, increasing the risk of health conditions from heart disease to depression, autoimmune disorders to addiction. This happens because trauma keeps our stress response systems in overdrive, flooding our bodies with cortisol and adrenaline long after the danger has passed, creating inflammation and dysregulation that can last decades. But there's the good news, too, as Dr. Nadine Burke Harris, California's first Surgeon General, has shown through her pioneering work, these effects aren't permanent. With the right support, including therapy, gentle meditation, exercise, nutrition, and adequate sleep, we can actually heal our nervous systems and reverse many of trauma's impacts. The body remembers trauma, yes, but it also has an extraordinary capacity to heal when given the right support and tools. I have been on a personal journey with this kind of healing, as you may have gathered. Every healing story is different, and I want to share a bit more of mine with you.

A gentle warning: the following mythic journey is about an inner process of healing, but includes themes of trauma and dismemberment as well as miraculous healing. If these themes are too hard to think about or uncomfortable for you right now, I want to honour that. Please skip over the following sections until you find a place that feels comfortable.

The Handless Maiden

The inner healing I've done has made a huge impact on these things for me. Not by bypassing them, but by learning to be gentle with myself, finding better ways to rest and look after myself, and finding ways to access and release old pain.

My journey of many years towards healing deeply buried psychological trauma, caused primarily by a very unsafe adult who was in my daily life thoughout my childhood has had many stages. It was influenced by working intentionally with the healing version of handless maiden's tale that Clarissa Pinkola Estés tells.

This was originally a Grim fairytale, which was based on older stories. Note that the "devil" in this story is not necessarily the Christian devil, rather, he is symbolic of our inner demons and saboteurs. Take a moment to sit with the story, remembering that we are every character in the story. Here is my version:

There was once a miller, poor and desperate, who was offered riched beyond his wildest dreams when a devil came to call. The devil asked for only whatever stood behind the mill. The miller thought of only his apple tree and agreed. But when he returned

SELF LOVE MAGIC 107

home, he found his daughter standing behind the mill, sweeping leaves.

When the devil came to collect, the girl had washed herself so clean with tears that he couldn't touch her. "Stop her from washing," he commanded. Still she remained pure. Every time the devil tried to take her, he was repelled by her innocence. Furious, the devil demanded: "Cut off her hands, or you will all perish." The father refused but the daughter offered up her own hands to save her family. The father wept, and took the axe to his daughter's wrists. But her innocent tears fell again and still the devil could not claim her. He left in fury.

The maiden could not stay. She knew she must leave. She wrapped her stumps and left home, walking until she came to a beautiful orchard at night. Starving, she saw golden pears hanging there. She walked up and ate, stretching up so her mouth could reach the fruit, juice running down her chin. The gardener thought he saw an ghost.

The king, furious about the theft of his pears, hid the next night and caught her. He recognised her essence and loved her instantly. He had silver hands made for her, married her with reverence. She bore a child. When war called him away, he left her in his mother's care.

The devil wasn't finished. He intercepted their letters, made the king's mother believe her son wanted his wife killed. Instead, she tied the baby to the young queen's back and sent her into the forest with sorrow and supplies.

Deep in the forest, she found an inn. The innkeeper, took her in. For seven years she lived there with her child, tending the hearth, learning the forest's ways. And slowly, like spring returning to winter ground, her hands grew back. Not silver. Not perfect. Her own flesh, lined and strong.

When the king returned and discovered the deception, he searched the world. Seven years he wandered until he too found the inn in the forest. At first, he didn't recognise this woman with her own hands, her quiet power. When she showed him her silver hands he believed, and then heunderstood: she'd become whole not through his protection but through her own long becoming.

Take a breath. Let the story settle in your bones. You've just witnessed an archetypal journey that maps the territory of wounding and healing, of what gets severed and what grows back. This isn't just a fairy tale, it's a map of a healing journey through trauma toward wholeness. Like all the old stories, it works on us beneath the level of logic, planting seeds in the unconscious, showing us patterns we've lived but perhaps never named. Now, let's trace the path this story illuminates, seeing how each stage might perhaps mirror our own journeys from wounding through to regeneration.

Processes and stages of healing

The handless maiden's tale maps the archetypal journey of wounding and regeneration. Bear in mind that healing isn't linear; it doesn't follow a straight line. Yet, through story, we see how innocence is betrayed, agency is lost, and wholeness is eventually reclaimed through endurance rather than rescue.

The Unconscious Bargain

The father archetype represents both external forces that harm us without meaning to, and the internal part that abandons our deeper knowing for promised relief. The devil is the shadow that drives toward destruction, offering seductive escapes that ultimately sabotage us. The maiden begins as innocence itself - trusting, undefended. In this stage, the father trades what he thinks is just an apple tree, for wealth. The father makes his deal without looking behind the mill. His unconscious bargain - wealth for an apple tree - reveals how we can unknowingly trade away what's precious while thinking we're being clever. The maiden stands behind the mill by chance, or perhaps by fate. The devil knows what the father refuses to see.

The Trauma

The father becomes the one who wounds despite loving, who chooses his survival over another's wholeness. The maiden, in her innocence, sacrifices herself but is protected by that very innocence. When the devil cannot take her, he demands her hands - her power and agency. She offers them to save her family. The severing removes her capacity to grasp, create, defend - the fundamental ability to shape her own life and yet she cannot stay and be coddled by her family. She knows she has her own life to live.

The Exile

The maiden now embodies the necessary exile, the one who cannot stay where betrayal happened. She must leave everything familiar and learn to survive without hands, unable to care for herself in human ways. This is the stripping down to essence. In this vulnerability she finds strength and begins to connect with her wildness. She is wounded, and feels the brokeness of her wounds, but underneath that pain she her essence is still strong, her intuition growing as she navigates the wilderness.

Soul Nourishment and Connection

The orchard symbolises the soul's mysterious ability to provide when all seems lost. The pears are grace itself - nourishment that comes through following the path of intuition. The maiden, starving, finds the fruit glows for her. She eats directly from the tree, face to fruit, in a primitive return to being fed by something greater than human provision.

The Alchemical Union

The king embodies the active spirit that recognises the deep soul of the maiden's wholeness, despite her wounds. This is an ancient alchemical concept of union between the active and receptice parts of the self. Through healing and uniting key parts of the self, the victim becomes the creator. In this inner-marriage, new life is conceived and born - new creations, possibilities, opportunities and dreams that lift us out of the prison of our old wounds. The gift of the silver hands represent the early attempts to replace what was lost. This conscious union plants seeds of wholeness. However, this is not the final transformation. The story does not end with this happily ever after because the king cannot save her. She must learn to heal herself.

The Story Continues

The child represents what we can now create from deepening our inner healing. Here the soul is trying to move forward but the journey is not yet complete. The devil returns as the force that won't let go of past pain and holds tight to the old bargain. Through twisted messages, the maiden is cast out again - now carrying more challenging responsibility. This second exile reflects how healing spirals; old wounds return just when we think we're safe. The mother-in-law who helps her flee shows how we can learn to have compassion for, protect, and nurture ourselves even when things get hard again.

The True Regeneration

The forest inn is the deep psyche where true healing happens. The innkeeper is the soul's own wisdom that knows how to tend us. Here the maiden becomes her own healing - not through rescue but through years of simple endurance. Her hands grow back slowly, season by season. They return scarred and real, not silver and perfect. Ultimately, she has to save herself, moment by moment, listening to nature and her own body. In this stillness and surrender, she is no longer a victim. The past trauma sheds from her like the leaves in autumn and though it takes time, that old pain breaks down into fertile compost to nourish the new growth of her deeper regeneration. Her hands, representing her power and agency, grow back and she is no longer the victimg of the past, she is now ready to be the active creator of her future.

Reunion and Integration

The king's seven-year search mirrors the maiden's regeneration - both the active spiritual principle and receptive soul must undergo parallel transformation to achieve true alchemical union. When they reunite, she has become sovereign creator - a queen in her own right - no longer the wounded maiden seeking salvation. He recognises her essence and she reveals her own authentic hands - no longer needing his gifted ones. The child, who has grown too, represents the fruit of spirit and soul united in full awareness. This is not rescue but recognition. The fulfillment of the inner-alchemical marriage is now possible because both principles have healed and grown through their own deep transformation.

After trauma severs our ability to grasp and shape the world, we can heal through nature, time and listening to our intuition, and learn different ways of being. We may not be able to literally grow back or recover from the limitations of this physical world, but in the inner healing, we can come back into wholeness and alignment that allows us to navigate our health and healing intuitively rather than as a self-perpetuating battle.

My inner mythic journey of healing

In my mid-twenties, feeling re-broken by academic failure, grief from the death of my grandfather, and heartbreak, I felt the subtle call of intuition. When visiting my grandmother, and sitting by the ocean, I felt it calling me home. I answered this call and moved to my grandparents' coastal town, to a house in the forest overlooking the ocean (and no, you do not need a literal forest to heal, this was a beautiful synchonicity). I moved with my young daughter and very little money. Over this time, I let go of my old life and most of the things I had owned and clung to. I discovered this healing story and many others and I worked with them actively. I realised that after many years of healing, I still had more to do, but I was already so far along the journey. I had already reached the forest. I had begun the process of transformation and nourishing myself. Now, I needed to do the deep work of the soul.

My body had shut down. The chronic fatigue and pain that had shadowed me since age twelve now consumed everything. But in that forest, I stopped fighting. I walked gently on the beach when I could. When I couldn't walk, I lay in the sand, letting my daughter play and trying not to cry too obviously. I soaked in the healing of the forest, breathing with the trees and connected with friends when I was able to. I surrendered my academic ambitions, my need to belong to my very academic family through achievement, the very things I had clung to as identity.

Slowly, like the handless maiden growing silver hands through years of forest healing, I began to transform. The pain didn't vanish, it eased as I listened and learned its language. The fatigue remained, but I found rhythms that honoured it. My body, which had felt so broken, began to feel like a wise teacher showing me a different way to live.

The forest time taught me what no academic degree could: how to release old pain stored in the body, how to trust the wisdom of rest, how to let the natural world hold what I couldn't carry. I faced my childhood wounds and released so much agonising emotion that my body shook in overwhelm. I shed many tears.

With very little but somehow enough, I lived between forest and ocean. My first Saturn return was coming - one of those formidable life transits - the one in our late twenties when learning happens, even though it's often hard. I journalled like my life depended on it and I surrendered. I let go of forcing life into familiar shapes. I handed my fate over to whatever larger forces were at work.

I let go…

As the healing continued, something shifted. I picked up the draft of a novel I had started but nad no idea how to finish. Encouraged by my stroppy therapist, Sherry, I put the tiny amount of regular time I could into this work (I had two hours in the afternoon of childcare during the week). Baby steps. I received a short email that changed my life. I discovered I still had access to a scholarship. I could do a PhD and research something I actually cared about. The path I thought was closed had quietly opened another way, and through the power of opening to my grief, I could embark on this journey with lightness and inspiration.

My wholeness grew back. I could touch life directly instead of through the numbing haze of pain. The forest time had worked its slow medicine. This healing led me to build a life and a career, out of what previously felt like total hopelessness and despair. I continued to heal while continuing my own writing and honouring my self.

This is how healing happens - not in straight lines but in spirals, returning again and again to tend what hurts until it transforms into strength.

Creating Rituals of Blessing

We need rituals that mark our body as sacred, not because it looks a certain way but because it's carried us through everything. Create a quiet space. Light a candle if you want, gather oils or objects that feel meaningful, but don't get lost in the accessories. The ritual is attention, not aesthetics.

Start with your feet. Actually touch them. Thank them for every step they've taken, every time they've carried you away from danger or toward what you love. Move upward slowly. Thank your legs for holding you up when you wanted to collapse. Thank your belly for its wisdom, even if you've spent years wishing it were different. Thank your heart for continuing to beat through every heartbreak. Thank your shoulders for carrying burdens that were sometimes not even yours. Thank your throat for every word spoken and swallowed. Thank your face for expressing what words couldn't.

This might feel ridiculous. You might cry. You might feel nothing at first. All responses are valid. The point is to spend time deliberately blessing what you've been taught to fix, deliberately honouring what you've learned to hide.

Why not take yourself on a date once a month or so? Walk barefoot on grass and actually feel it. Take a bath with flowers or salts or nothing special except your full attention. Dance alone in your living room to music that makes you feel alive. Eat a meal slowly enough to taste it. Get a massage or give yourself one, approaching your body as beloved rather than problem.

This is the art of building a relationship with the body you actually have, not the one you think you should have. After each date with yourself, write a brief note to your body. Nothing elaborate, maybe just "Thank you for showing up today" or "I'm learning to listen to you" or "We're doing this together." These small acknowledgments build trust over time.

The Soul of the Body

John O'Donohue wrote that the body is a faithful friend of the soul. But most of us treat it like an inconvenient stranger, something to manage rather than inhabit. The deeper magic happens when we realise the body holds truths the mind can't access. Your shoulders know about burdens in ways your thoughts never will. Your belly understands intuition before your brain catches up. Your heart has its own intelligence about love and loss.

When you live from your body instead of despite it, you live from truth. The mind can rationalise anything. Culture can shame you into any shape. But the body remembers what's real. It knows when you're safe and when you're not. It knows when you're lying to yourself. It knows when you're coming home.

You weren't meant to be at war with yourself, policing your hunger, punishing your desires, hiding your scars. You were meant to be in conversation with this flesh that's carried you through everything. In wonder at its persistence. In gratitude for its patience as you learn, finally, to stop abandoning the one home you'll have from birth to death.

The temple was always yours. The sacred was always here. In your breath, in your heartbeat, in the body you're sitting in right now, reading these words. Come home. Not because you should, but because you can. Because your body has been waiting for you all along, faithful as gravity, patient as earth. Ready whenever you are.

When you truly inhabit your body, you become ungovernable in the best way. You can't be sold solutions to problems that don't exist. You can't be convinced you're broken when you feel your wholeness. You can't be controlled through shame when you're rooted in your own sensation.

You Are Already Home

"You do not have to be good.
You do not have to walk on your knees
for a hundred miles through the desert, repenting.
You only have to let the soft animal of your body

love what it loves.
Tell me about despair, yours, and I will tell you mine.
Meanwhile the world goes on.
Meanwhile the sun and the clear pebbles of the rain
are moving across the landscapes,
over the prairies and the deep trees,
the mountains and the rivers.
Meanwhile the wild geese, high in the clean blue air,
are heading home again.
Whoever you are, no matter how lonely,
the world offers itself to your imagination,
calls to you like the wild geese, harsh and exciting –
over and over announcing your place
in the family of things."
— Mary Oliver

As Mary Oliver wrote, you do not have to be good. You can simply let the soft animal of your body love what it loves.

Your body never left you. It kept breathing you through panic attacks. It kept your heart beating through heartbreak. It carried you through everything, even your abandonment of it. It has loved you through every size, every age, every ability, every change. It has been your most faithful companion, your longest relationship, your first and final home.

The path back isn't about fixing your body. It's about fixing your relationship with it. It's about saying: I'm sorry I left. I'm here now. Thank you for waiting. Thank you for everything. You are not a mind driving a meat robot. You are not a spirit trapped in a body. You are a magnificent integration of matter and consciousness, a miracle of aliveness, a walking temple of the sacred.

You ARE the altar. You are the temple. You are the sacred space where body and spirit meet. Welcome home to your body. Welcome home to your senses. Welcome home to the wisdom you've always carried, the pleasure you deserve, the presence that changes everything. Your body has been waiting for this reunion. And now, finally, you're here.

Place both hands over your heart. Feel the beat that has never forgotten you: "I'm home. Thank you for waiting. I'm home."

7

EMBODIED BOUNDARIES AS ACTS OF LOVE

Feel the edges of your skin right now. Notice where you end and the world begins. This boundary, this meeting place between self and other, is your first teacher in the sacred art of differentiation. Run your fingertips along your arm and feel how clearly your body knows its own borders. This knowing lives in every cell. You were born with boundaries intact. The question is: when did you learn to abandon them?

There's a story we need to excavate here, and like all the fairy tales we've been exploring, it lives in your body as much as your memory.

Your body remembers every boundary that was crossed. The memories live in your tissues, creating what we might call a boundary map of your history. Stan Tatkin's research into the neurobiology of relationships reveals that our nervous systems are constantly scanning: *Safe or unsafe? Approach or retreat?* When our boundaries are crossed, even subtly, the body registers threat. That tightness when someone stands too close? That's your body saying, "This isn't okay."

But trauma can scramble these signals. If saying no meant abandonment, your body might freeze instead of signalling. If having needs meant shame, you might feel anxiety when attempting the smallest boundary. This is why boundary work is really nervous system work, creating enough safety to feel our authentic responses again.

Think of someone who consistently drains you. Notice what happens in your body just thinking about them. Does your chest tighten? Stomach clench? Energy drop? Now think of someone who respects your boundaries. Feel the difference? Your body knows things your mind might still be figuring out.

Boundaries are like the thorns of the soul's rose. They're not there to hurt but to protect what's tender and beautiful within. Without thorns, roses would be devoured. Sometimes our old boundaries do indeed hurt us, because we are stuck in storied of pain from the past. Sometimes they need to be pruned away for the new growth for come through. Sometimes they share important truths with us about what we *do* actually want.

The Water Women's Teaching

In the oldest stories of water women, selkies of the Scottish isles, nixies of the German rivers, the rusalka of Slavic lakes, there lives a deep teaching about boundaries. These beings could move between water and land, but they always kept their way home. The selkie hid her seal skin. The swan maiden kept her feather cloak. They knew that to love on land, they needed to protect their return to water.

By the time Hans Christian Andersen retold the little mermaid, the story had shifted into something more sinister. The mermaid willingly lets the sea witch cut out her tongue in a devil's bargain. She trades her voice and one of her most powerful senses for painful legs, for proximity to a prince who doesn't even recognise her as the one who saved him.

This is how we sever our boundaries, through a thousand small cuts in the hopes that we will somehow exchange them for love and acceptance. The child who says "I don't want to hug him" and hears "Don't be rude." The woman who expresses discomfort and is told she's "too sensitive." Each override teaches us to distrust our own tongue, our own taste for what's true and our ability to speak up for ourselves.

But the older stories hold medicine. When the selkie finally finds her hidden skin, after years of searching every corner, every locked chest, she either slips back into the sea to finally live for herself or she negotiates so that she can live in both worlds. She shows her children their dual heritage, teaches them that love includes letting people be what they are.

The little mermaid is offered something similar, a knife from her sisters to cut herself free from the bargain that's killing her. The same blade that severed her tongue could sever the contract. But she chooses to dissolve instead, to become foam at the boundary between sea and shore. We owe it to ourselves not to become such a tragic tale.

Our boundaries are part of our way home to ourselves. When we can't say no, we lose our ability to taste what's true. When we give up our essential nature for a sense of acceptance or in the hopes of being loved, we start to fade. Love that requires our silence and the sacrifice of our inner wildness is not really love at all, it is imprisonment. But the return is always possible. We do not return to who we were before but to a wiser self who knows that real love makes room for all of us, including our own inner depths.

Make a list of the things you've never said for fear of getting hurt or hurting people. So you have one close friend you could share these things with? Who you could ask to listen without judgement? Speaking these things aloud, even when alone, is powerful magic; sharing them with someone you trust is even more potent.

Why Boundaries Feel Like Betrayal

Let me name what haunts most of us when we consider boundaries: the terror of being called selfish. In my body, this word carries the weight of exile. To be selfish is to be cast out from belonging, to confirm our worst fears about our unworthiness of love.

The people who are most upset by your boundaries are often those who benefited most from your lack of them.

When you start having boundaries, you're disrupting their convenience and they might not like it, but respecting your own boundaries is important.

Every no contains information about what you need to say yes to, even if that yes is simply to your own need for rest, space, or sovereignty. You don't need elaborate explanations to justify your needs, you simply need to get clear on what they are, and let other people know. In this way, you can become a strong guardian for your own boundaries.

When you learned as a child that saying no meant violence, physical, emotional, or the violence of withdrawal, your nervous system remembers. The thought of setting a boundary can trigger the same physiological response as facing a predator.

This is your body trying to keep you safe using old programming. If compliance meant survival, your body will choose compliance even when the danger has passed. If being boundaryless secured attachment, your nervous system will override your adult knowledge that you're allowed to have needs.

This is why we must go slowly…

- Starting with the smallest possible no (maybe just "I need to think about that")
- Practicing with safe people first
- Having a support plan for after you set a boundary
- Celebrating tiny victories (you paused before saying yes!)

- Working with your body to create new neural pathways of safety

Your body is trying to protect you. Thank it for its vigilance while gently updating its programming.

The Art of Disappointing Others

This might sound harsh, but you are going to disappoint people. This is not a flaw in your boundary practice, it's proof that it's working. You cannot live an authentic life without sometimes disappointing others' expectations of you. It's a bitter saturnian pill to swallow but the cold hard reality is that we can't always please everyone, and we certainly can't be empowered by trying. At times, either you disappoint others by having boundaries, or you disappoint yourself by abandoning them.

You are not responsible for other people's expectations or their disappointment. Learning to tolerate others' disappointment is like building a muscle. At first, even the smallest sigh from someone you've said no to feels unbearable. Your whole system screams to take it back, fix it, make them happy again. But each time you survive someone's disappointment, you build capacity. You learn that their feelings are not your emergency.

We talk about boundaries as if they only exist between us and others, but some of our most important boundaries are internal. Boundaries with our own thoughts, patterns, and behaviours that no longer serve us. Sometimes we need boundaries:

- With the tendency to spiral into worst-case scenarios
- With checking work emails at midnight
- With scrolling when we needed sleep
- With comparing ourselves to others
- With abandoning the body's needs for the sake of "productivity"

These internal boundaries require the same practice as external ones. Notice the urge. Pause. Choose differently. Not from self-punishment but from self-protection.

The Victim Shadow of Boundaries

There's a shadow side to boundary work. It's easy to slip into using the sacred language of self-protection to avoid the messy work of self-examination. "You crossed my boundary!" we can say, hurling accusations at people we care about because we don't like the way they are protecting their own boundaries.

For many years, I kept falling into the same painful patterns with relationships. Each time thinking this infatuation would save me, each time learning it couldn't. Slowly I understood: I was projecting my own unhealed pain onto the other, just as they projected theirs onto me. The emotions that felt so huge, so tied to another person, were actually mine to reclaim.

When I let go of this, years of held grief moved through me like water, and in that release I knew something clearly: I wasn't broken at my core. I'd felt broken, lived with that feeling so long it seemed like truth. But underneath, something had always remained whole.

To be transparent, I still fall into painful projections in relationship. When I feel unsafe, uncared for or unheard, when big emotions like anxiety, terror, and pain surface, I look outside myself for the source, and sometimes a boundary I'm holding has not been respected, or a need I have is unmet. Sometimes the other person has done something hurtful, yes, but there's also an inner truth to be learned and old emotion to be healed. I tend to feel such big emotion because an old wound is triggered. I'm much quicker at identifying my patterns so that my pain can lead me to deeper healing, and the old patterns continue to evolve and change into healthier new ones, reflected in new and more empowered stories, rather than repeating the old ones over and over.

When are boundaries are crossed, we feel victimised. When we are the victim, it's hard to be an active creator of our own experience. Herein lies the paradox.

I've watched this shadow consume people. The person who cuts off anyone who challenges them, calling it "boundary setting." The one who labels every difficult emotion as "trauma response" without examining their own patterns. The friend who uses "I'm an empath" to justify why everyone else's energy is always wrong, never considering what they're contributing to the dynamic.

This shadow is particularly seductive because it wears the costume of healing. We get to feel righteous in our self-protection. We get to avoid the discomfort of seeing our own sharp edges, our own difficult behaviours, our own contributions to painful dynamics. We become the perpetual victim in our own fairy tale, wanting others to rescue us, never noticing we've become the villain in someone else's story at the very same time that they have become the same in ours.

The medicine is discernment. Real boundaries include the boundary with our own victim mentality. When we feel the familiar rise of "my boundaries are being crossed," we can learn to pause and ask:

- Is this genuinely violating my limits, or is it touching something I need to examine?
- Am I protecting my peace or avoiding my growth?
- Is this person really toxic, or are they reflecting something I don't want to see? (both can be true)
- Am I using boundary language to shut down feedback I need to hear?

Sometimes the answer is yes, this is a real violation that needs a firm boundary. But sometimes, more often than the inner-victim wants to admit, it's an invitation to look at what we are projecting, avoiding, or refusing to own.

This work includes being willing to lower the drawbridge sometimes, to let in the feedback that stings because it's true, to admit that not everyone who hurts us is an enemy. Some are teachers. Some are mirrors. Some are showing us where we still need to grow.

The Sacred Fire of Righteous Rage

There's such a thing as righteous rage, as my friend, Talia Marshall who is a talented writer reflected, when she gave me editorial feedback on this book. There's something powerful about rage, particularly the kind that rises when it feels like boundaries have been decimated, when someone has taken what was never theirs to take. This rage is not something to be ashamed of or to spiritually bypass with premature forgiveness. Your fury at violation is sacred truth. It's the part of you that knows you deserved better, the guardian that would have protected you if it could. Some things deserve our rage. Some violations warrant fury. The question isn't whether you should feel it, but whether you'll let it teach you about your worth, let it forge you into someone who will never again apologise for having boundaries made of iron and fire.

When rage rises, let it. As I suggest in Chapter Four, you can find safe ways to move it through your body - pound pillows, scream into the void, write uncensored letters you'll never send, dance until you're sweating out the poison. Your rage says: I matter and I always mattered. And anyone who taught me otherwise was wrong. This fury is information, it's your nervous system's navigation showing you where your sovereignty was violated, and perhaps where you learned to betray yourself to keep others comfortable.

The Hidden Gift in Boundaries

Every no contains a yes. Kasia Urbaniak teaches that when we're clear about what we're rejecting, we discover what we're protecting, what we actually want. It's not enough to know what we're against - we need to feel into what we're for.

When you say "It's not okay that my mother dismisses my feelings," what are you saying yes to? Perhaps you're saying yes to relationships where your emotional reality is honoured. When you declare "I won't tolerate being spoken to that way," you're saying yes to dignity, to respect, to conversations that uplift rather than diminish. The boundary isn't just a wall, it's a doorway to what you actually desire.

Take a moment with your rage. Let it burn hot and bright. Then ask: What is this rage protecting? What would I actually say yes to instead? Maybe your no to being constantly available is a yes to rest, to presence, to having a self outside of service. Maybe your no to criticism is a yes to environments where you can bloom without fear. The rage shows you where the violation lives, yes. But underneath the rage is the desire for something better that honours who you actually are. Focusing on that is far more energising and empowering.

Liberation Without Forgiveness

I have personally found forgiveness work to be healing, but it took me such a long time to get there and I'm going to tell you something a bit controvercial: You don't have to forgive the unforgivable. You don't have to make peace with cruelty or find the lesson in someone else's violence.

Forgiveness is not a requirement for your healing. In her podcast, You Make Sense, somatic therapist Sarah Baldwin, having suffered tremendous abuse herself, makes this powerful point. You do not always need to forgive in order to heal, but you can still release yourself from the past, regardless (as an aside, I recommend Sarah's work as a powerful path to healing and regulating the nervous system, It is filled with so much wisdom.)

You can honour the "no" that says it wasn't okay, and still set yourself free. You can do is release yourself from carrying the poison in your bloodstream from the person who hurt you. You can release yourself from the hold those people might have on you emotionally, accepting that bad things did happen and you weren't cared for in the way you should have been. You can release the past, and maybe…just maybe, you can get the the point of forgiving life for containing such cruelty.

Rage is fire, and fire can destroy or transform. The rage that burns everything, including you, is one thing. But rage that burns clean is passion. It can fuel your healthy boundary-setting, clear communication and, your refusal to accept less than respect. You can honour your commitment to protecting yourself now in ways you couldn't then. That's medicine.

Setting yourself free doesn't mean pretending it was okay. It means taking back your life force from the past, reclaiming the energy you've spent reliving the violation. It means saying: "What you did was wrong. It will always be wrong. And I'm no longer organising my life around your wrongness. I release the past. I accept that I cannot change it but that I can reclaim my power now. I set myself free.

You can acknowledge the wound, honour the scar, and still choose to stop drinking poison while waiting for them to die from it, as many wise teachers have advised. Your freedom isn't contingent on their apology, their understanding, or their transformation. Your freedom lives in claiming your right to build a life on your own terms.

Boundary Affirmations

Write these in your journal. Say them to your reflection. Let them live in your body until they become truth:

- ☐ I approve of my needs
- ☐ I trust my no
- ☐ I trust my yes
- ☐ I am safe to have boundaries
- ☐ I choose myself with love
- ☐ I honour my energy
- ☐ I am allowed to rest
- ☐ I listen to my body
- ☐ I am worthy of respect
- ☐ I am allowed to change
- ☐ I trust my knowing

☐ I belong to myself

☐ I am safe to be myself

☐ I respect my boundaries

☐ I choose healthy connections

☐ I am my own guardian

☐ I trust my timing

Gentle ways to communicate boundaries:

When you need time to feel into your truth: "I need to check with myself before I commit. I'll let you know by [specific time]."

When someone is emotionally dumping: "I care about what you're going through, and I don't have the capacity to hold this right now. Can we talk about it [suggest specific later time] when I have more bandwidth?"

When receiving unsolicited advice: "I appreciate you thinking of me. I'm finding my own way with this."

When someone guilt-trips you: "I hear that you're disappointed. This is still what I need to do."

When someone tests a boundary you've already set: "We talked about this. My answer hasn't changed."

For invasive questions: "I'm not up for discussing that." (Then change the subject, you don't owe explanation)

When someone needs immediate response: "I can't give you an answer right now. If you need to know immediately, I'll have to say no."

The Ripple Effect

As you strengthen your boundaries, notice the ripples. Some relationships will deepen, the people who truly love you will celebrate your self-care, even if it takes adjustment. They've been waiting for you to show up fully, not as a depleted shell but as a whole person.

Other relationships will reveal themselves. The friend who only called when they needed something. The family member who required your self-abandonment to feel secure. The colleague who mistook your lack of boundaries for invitation to take advantage.

This sorting can be painful. You might grieve relationships you thought were nourishing but were actually draining. You might feel guilty about protecting your peace. Remember: guilt is often the price of growth. It's the old programming protesting the new way.

Most beautifully, your boundaries give others permission. When you model what it looks like to honour your limits with love, you become a walking invitation. Your children learn they're allowed to have needs. Your friends remember they can say no. Your community begins to explore what sustainable care actually looks like.

Living Inside Your Own Skin

As boundaries become integrated, they stop feeling like something you do and become something you are. You don't have to think about them constantly because they've become as natural as breathing. Your yes means yes. Your no means no. Your maybe means you'll truly consider.

You become someone who can love deeply without losing yourself, give generously without depleting yourself, connect authentically without betraying yourself. You discover that boundaries don't limit love, they make it possible. They're the riverbanks that let love flow in its power without flooding everything in its path. Your boundaries are not mean or cruel or selfish. They're the architecture of a life where everyone's humanity is honoured, starting with your own.

Feel your edges again. The boundary of your skin. The space you're allowed to claim. This is your territory, and you are its loving guardian. Every limit you honour is enchantment towards a world where we can meet each other in wholeness and love.

8

SELF-LOVE IN RELATIONSHIP

Place one hand on your heart and the other reaching outward, palm open. Feel the pulsing life beneath your first hand, your own centre, your sovereign self. Feel the space and possibility in your extended hand, the capacity for connection with others. From a state of self-love, centred in our own being, we are in a better place for connecting with others, lovingly, and feeling loved in return.

Many of us grow up believing that the right person would finally make us feel worthy of love, and why wouldn't we? This trope is so common in popular culture, in songs and movies and books that it's ingrained in us from an early age. But what we have been taught is the essence of romance is actually a romance narrative trap.

This is not to say we can't be loved wonderfully and beautifully, that we can't have fulfilling relationships, it's just that we cannot find inner fulfilment purely through an external source. The old adage is true – to feel fulfilled in love from another we often have to love ourselves first, truly and deeply. Many of us think that if someone special chooses us, it will prove we are choosable. If someone stays, it means we are worth staying for. From this wonky perspective we give our partners an impossible job: to convince us of our worth when we fundamentally don't believe in it ourselves. But, of course, this can be changed, and in this book, we are already on the path towards that change.

As Esther Perell says, "Today, we turn to one person to provide what an entire village once did: a sense of grounding, meaning, and continuity. At the same time, we expect our committed relationships to be romantic as well as emotionally and sexually fulfilling. Is it any wonder that so many relationships crumble under the weight of it all?" In doing this work, we can free our partners from the enormous and impossible romantic burden of being everything to us. We free ourselves from the constant disappointment of heavy expectations, and open up to new inner resources that can help us have much more satisfying relationships.

Everything changes when we bring self-love to relationship. Not perfection, none of us arrive at partnership fully healed, completely whole, beyond our wounds. But when we've done the work of the previous chapters, when we can approve of ourselves, when we are prepared to face our shadows as they arise, when we're learning to inhabit our bodies and hold our boundaries, we bring a different quality of presence to intimacy.

The shift is subtle but significant. Instead of seeking someone to complete us, we seek someone to share our wholeness with. Instead of needing someone to heal our wounds, we take responsibility for our own healing while allowing another to witness and support. Instead of losing ourselves in merger, we practice what psychologists call **differentiation**, clear acceptance of ourselves and our partners as different people, not tangled up in one merged identity, and **individuation**, the ability to be stay connected to ourselves while being close to the other.

From Scarcity to Abundance

Have you experienced a feeling of scarcity when it comes to love? When I was younger and felt emotionally broken, there's never enough love, attention or validation to fill the void inside. I was like a hungry ghost, no matter how much my partners gave, it disappeared into the bottomless pit of my unworthiness. I needed a lot of reassurance. I interpreted every moment of distance as abandonment. I shapeshifted endlessly, trying to become whatever I thought they wanted.

I would pursue anxiously when I sensed distance. My partners would withdraw from the intensity of my need. I would pursue harder. They would withdraw further. Round and round we went, each of us confirming our worst fears about love. If my partner happened to be more excited about the relationship than I was, I'd go into the opposite pattern. Instead of anxiously seeking their validation, I'd push them away and they'd anxiously seek my attention until even being in the same room made me feel ill.

But as I began to fill my own well through self-love practices, doing the work of healing myself, something shifted. I stopped needing my partner to be my only source of nourishment. I developed the ability to self-soothe, to tolerate relationship uncertainty, to trust in connection even during conflict.

When we love ourselves, we approach relationship from abundance rather than deficit. We have love to give because we're open to it flowing through us, not just from our partner, but from the infinite source of all things that almost every spiritual tradition shares glimpses of, the fundamental truth that beyond the limits of this world and the limitations we experience in life there is a deep, overflowing, universal love. From this place, we can be generous because we're not depleted. We can allow our partners their full humanity because we're allowing our own.

When we don't love ourselves, we try to squeeze ourselves into different shapes to become whoever we think others want us to be. We abandon our opinions, preferences, needs, desires. We become relationship chameleons, changing our colours to match whoever we're with. It takes courage to be honest about who we truly are and what we really want, but it is ultimately rewarding. The exhaustion of maintaining these false selves is crushing, but not as crushing as the loneliness of never being truly known.

The powerful feminist writer who needs no capitalisation, bell hooks, wrote that "Knowing how to be solitary is central to the art of loving. When we can be alone, we can be with others without using them as a means of escape." This solitude, not isolation, but sovereignty, is what self-love teaches us. When we can be alone without loneliness, we can be with others without losing ourselves.

Navigating Conflict from Love

Conflict in relationship is inevitable. But when we're rooted in self-love, conflict transforms from a threat to an opportunity. Instead of seeing disagreement as evidence that we're unlovable or the relationship is doomed, we can approach it with what Terry Real calls "relational mindfulness."

This means staying connected to ourselves during conflict. Noticing when we're flooded and need a break. Speaking from our experience rather than attacking our partner's character. Taking responsibility for our part without taking responsibility for everything. Repair becomes more important than being right.

I remember my first conscious conflict after beginning this work. My partner had done something that hurt me. Old me would have either exploded in rage or suppressed the hurt entirely. But I had been practicing. I noticed the hurt in my body. I took time to understand what was happening for me. Then I approached them: "When you did X, I felt Y. Can we talk about it?"

No blame. No character assassination. No threat of abandonment. Just clear communication from a place of self-respect. My partner was able to hear me because I wasn't attacking. I was able to listen too, because I wasn't desperate for the other to validate my worth. We found our way through conflicts more easily as we learned these skills, and the relationship deepened.

Attachment and Wholeness

Stan Tatkin's work on attachment shows that we unconsciously choose partners who confirm our core beliefs about ourselves and relationships. When we believe we're unworthy, we choose partners who treat us as unworthy, not because we're masochistic, but because it feels familiar. It confirms what we "know" to be true.

When we struggle with anxious attachment in relationship, we project our anxiety onto the other person. The problem is that attachment wounds tend to originate in early childhood when our needs aren't met. The other person isn't responsible for causing the pattern with us, and can't reach into our past and stop the pain, neither can they resolve the anxiety when they trigger it. It might seem like they are the problem, and they might indeed be doing something problematic, but the pattern itself is ours. The anxiety is ours, and when we project it onto another person, they can't make it go away, not fully. Sure they could try to reassure us, change their behaviour and tiptoe around our fear and pain, hoping to never trigger it again, but it will remain within us, waiting to be triggered again unless we can learn how to face it ourselves.

Anxious patterns tend to be exacerbated by avoidant patterns and vice versa. If we push our partners away, they will likely become more anxious. Both these patterns come from disconnections in our childhoods, and most people struggle with these to some extent at points in their lives. Even people who usually have secure relationship patterns can suddenly experience insecure attachments for the first time in a situation where their partner is not meeting their expectations in certain ways that make them feel hurt or fearful.

Self-love is a powerful remedy to this. When we can learn to take care of our vulnerable parts first, the other people close to us can assist us better and we can communicate more clearly, not from the overwhelmed pain of the small child within us who has all kinds of stories of how we are being mistreated, but from a broader view where we can hold our own vulnerability and feel our feelings, love and nurture ourselves, and then share and communicate more constructively about what we want and need. From this place, our partners are more able to support us without being triggered into their own overwhelming pain and fear.

When we love ourselves, we choose and relate to partners differently. We're not looking for someone to heal us, complete us, or save us. We're looking for someone to grow alongside, to witness and be witnessed by, to create with. Our relationships evolve so that our partners begin to:

- Respect our boundaries rather than pushing against them
- Celebrate our growth rather than feeling threatened by it
- Have their own self-love practice rather than needing us to be their only source
- Can tolerate intimacy without consuming us
- See relationship as a place to give rather than just get

This doesn't mean we're only attracted to "perfect" people. It means we're attracted to people whose imperfections are workable with ours, whose growth edges complement our own, whose capacity for love matches what we're ready to receive and give.

The Magic of Interdependence

Esther Perel speaks of this as the essential paradox of intimacy: "Love enjoys knowing everything about you; desire needs mystery. Love likes to shrink the distance that exists between me and you, while desire is energised by it." But this paradox only works when we're not using relationship to escape ourselves. When we're rooted in self-love, we can tolerate the space between self and other. We can be intimate without fusion, connected without consumption.

True intimacy requires what psychologists call interdependence, a state where two whole people choose to interweave their lives while maintaining their individual identities. This is different from independence (I don't need anyone) or codependence (I can't exist without you). It's a third way: I am whole, you are whole, and together we create something beautiful.

Interdependence looks like:

- Maintaining your own friendships, interests, and practices
- Supporting each other's growth even when it's uncomfortable
- Being able to self-soothe while also accepting comfort
- Sharing feelings without making your partner responsible for them
- Celebrating each other's autonomy as well as your connection

This requires constant calibration. Sometimes we lean into connection. Sometimes we need more autonomy. The key is that both movements come from choice rather than compulsion, from love rather than fear.

When Self-Love Challenges Partnership

When you begin to truly love yourself, some relationships become unsustainable; The partner who needed you to stay small feels threatened by your growth; The dynamic that worked when you had no boundaries falls apart when you start having needs; The connection that felt like love when you were self-abandoning reveals itself as addiction.

This can be heartbreaking. I've watched friends outgrow marriages that required their diminishment. It's hard, but sometimes a relationship ending is a blessing in the end. And not every ending of a romantic partnership is a failure, after all, there isn't really an end-goal in life or relationships. Sometimes romance transforms into friendship in the quiet recognition that you are both growing in different directions. From a position grounded in self-love, you can thank each other for your time and learning together, grieve the loss of old dreams to clear space for new things to grow in your lives, and move on with appreciation and love. Endings can be painful, and sometimes we just know that we need to let go. It's scary to leave what is known and face the fear of the unknown, but sometimes our soul is calling for it, and resisting that call can become even more painful over time.

Something else can happen when we do this work; relationships can deepen and transform when both people commit to their own growth. It is magical and powerful when partners can use each other's expansion as inspiration for their own. In this process we can experience love that grows stronger as each person becomes more themselves.

The key is discernment. Is your partner threatened by your self-love, or just adjusting to the change? Are they willing to grow alongside you, or invested in you staying the same? Can the relationship expand to hold who you're becoming, or has it become too small?

Loving Others While Loving Yourself

Some people worry that self-love will make them selfish in relationships. If I prioritise my needs, won't I neglect my partner? If I maintain boundaries, won't intimacy suffer? If I stop squeezing myself to fit, will anyone love the real me?

But the opposite is true. When we love ourselves, we have more love to give. When we maintain our boundaries, we can be truly present rather than resentfully compliant. When we show up as ourselves, we allow for real intimacy rather than connection based on performance.

Would you rather receive a gift from someone who gives from abundance or obligation? Would you rather be loved by someone who chooses you freely or needs you desperately? Would you rather make love with someone present in their body or disconnected from themselves?

Self-love enhances our capacity to love others because:

- We're not using them to fill our emptiness
- We can see them clearly rather than through projection
- We have energy to give because we're not depleted
- We can celebrate their wholeness because we're claiming our own
- We can navigate conflict because we're not terrified of abandonment

The Sacred Mirror of Relationship

Here's a question I've always found helpful: what are you learning from these relationships? Harville Hendrix teaches that we unconsciously choose partners who reflect our unfinished business. They trigger our core wounds not to hurt us but to heal us, if we're willing to do the work. In this way, relationships can act as sacred mirrors, showing us where we still abandon ourselves, where we still project our shadow, where we still seek external salvation.

When I was younger, I would fall into infatuation at the drop of a hat, and fall out of it just as quickly. I'd meet someone and not even like them at first, then, somehow, I'd feel that spark of chemistry, and quickly go into that exciting rush of symbiosis or merging – that first stage of relationships where everything feels wonderful. Over the course of 1-3 months I'd lose myself in the other person, feeling I was absolutely in love with them, dreaming big dreams complete with grand romantic gestures. Then, the bubble would burst and I'd realise my first instinct was correct: I didn't really like the person after all! (How embarrassing) Why? Why was this happening? Did I really have such poor judgement? After a while I realised that I was drawn to people who reflected deep wounds that I, myself, needed to heal within me. In every one of these relationships I was learning something important about myself, and so was the other person.

In feeling broken myself, I used to feel attracted to other broken people. You know, the broody mysterious ones? It wasn't until the end of my 20s, and the powerful healing work of my Saturn Return, where I had healed my inner foundation well enough that I stopped being attracted to broken people and started to have healthy relationships. The learning hasn't stopped, and in fact, the healing has only deepened over time, because this is a life-long journey, but in the process, my relationships have become much more satisfying and wonderful, including friendships and my relationship with parenting, it's all connected.

When we're practicing self-love, we can use this mirror consciously. When our partner triggers us, instead of just reacting, we can ask: What is this showing me about myself? Where am I still seeking from them what I need to give myself? What shadow is being reflected back to me?

This doesn't mean taking responsibility for everything or bypassing real relationship issues. It means approaching relationship as a crucible for growth, a sacred container where both people can become more whole.

When both partners are committed to self-love, you can create practices that support individual and relational growth:

- Start the day with individual practice (meditation, journaling, movement) before coming together. This ensures you're meeting from fullness rather than need.
- Create structured time to share what's alive for each of you individually and relationally. This prevents unconscious distance or merger.

- Develop agreements about how you'll handle conflict, when to pause, how to repair, what support you each need.
- Regularly appreciate both each other AND yourselves. Model self-love for each other.
- Explicitly discuss and respect each other's boundaries. Celebrate them as acts of self-love rather than rejection.

Self-Love in All Our Connections

The sacred mirror of relationship doesn't exist only in romance. Our children, parents, siblings, and friends all reflect back to us the places where we've abandoned ourselves, where old wounds still throb, where we react from pain rather than respond from love.

I discovered this most painfully through parenting. Nothing, and I mean nothing, has triggered my unhealed wounds quite like my child. The first time my toddler screamed "I hate you!" something primal rose in me. Not just hurt, but rage. How dare this tiny person I'd sacrificed everything for speak to me like that?

At times like this, it's important to take a moment, even if it's two minutes locked in the bathroom. There, sitting on the closed toilet lid, I let myself feel what was really happening. Beneath the rage was a devastated inner child, the one who'd tried so hard to be good, to earn love, to never cause trouble. My child's rejection had touched that ancient wound of powerlessness and not being lovable enough.

I let the tears come, knowing that my child was having their own big feelings and didn't have better words yet. They were doing exactly what I was doing, feeling overwhelmed and lashing out.

Through this, I could see them clearly. Not as my persecutor but as a small person drowning in emotion. This is the work that my dear great aunt, Ruth Beaglehole, dedicated her life to, in her work on compassionate parenting and education, teaching people to connect with children in empathy: "Those are big feelings," Ruth would say. "Hard feelings." "It's okay to be angry."

Magic happens when we can tend our own wounds first, then we can tend to others' without making them responsible for our pain. When we parent our inner children, we can parent our actual children from wholeness rather than wound. When we hold space for our own big feelings, we can hold space for theirs. When we practice self-compassion, we model what it looks like to be human without shame.

The same principle applies to every relationship that triggers us. When your mother makes that comment about your weight and you feel yourself shrinking back into the criticised child, that's your cue. Not to attack or defend, but to pause. To feel where it lands in your body. To ask: what part of me is hurting right now? What does she need?

When your friend cancels plans again and you feel that familiar abandonment rising, before you send the passive-aggressive text, stop. Feel the disappointment and notice if it's touching older disappointments. Tend to the part of you that feels forgotten before you respond. From that tended place, you might still need to have a conversation about reliability, but it will come from clarity rather than old pain.

Our most difficult relationships are often our greatest teachers. A teenager's eye rolls touch our fear of not being respected. A parent's anxiety activates our childhood hypervigilance. A friend's success triggers our scarcity fears. Each trigger is an invitation: will you react from wound or respond from wholeness?

The practice looks like this:

Pause: When you feel the emotional charge rising, stop. Even if it's just for three breaths.

Locate: Where do you feel it in your body? Chest tight? Stomach churning? Throat closing?

Ask: What age does this feeling remind me of? Often our biggest triggers touch our earliest wounds.

Tend: Speak to that wounded part like you would a frightened child. "I see this is really hard. You're safe now. I've got you."

Clarify: What's actually happening in this present moment, separate from the old story?

Respond: From this tended place, how do you want to show up? What would love do here?

This doesn't mean becoming a doormat or bypassing real issues. Sometimes love looks like fierce boundaries. Sometimes it looks like difficult conversations. But when we tend to our wounds first, we can have those conversations from strength rather than reactivity, from self-love rather than self-abandonment.

In this, every relationship becomes an opportunity for deeper healing. Our children teach us about our own inner children. Our parents show us where we still seek external approval. Our friends reflect our relationship with ourselves. And as we tend to each trigger with compassion, as we parent our own wounded parts, we become capable of love that isn't contingent on others being different. We can love them in their messiness because we've learned to love our own.

This is how self-love ripples outward, not by making us perfect, but by making us present to our own pain so we don't unconsciously pass it on. The world needs this kind of love, the kind that can hold complexity, that can see beneath behaviour to pain, that can respond rather than react. It begins in that pause, that sacred moment when you choose to feel your feelings and hold yourself in love before you act. It begins with becoming your own good parent, your own best friend, your own sacred witness. From that foundation, every relationship transforms.

The Integration of Love

As self-love deepens, the distinction between self-love and other-love begins to dissolve. Not into codependent merger, but into a unified field of love for life. You love yourself, so you can love others. You love others, which reinforces your self-love. The love circulates and multiplies.

This is what Thich Nhat Hanh points to when he speaks of "interbeing", the recognition that we are interconnected with everything. Your self-love contributes to the field of love available to all beings. Your partner's self-love nourishes you. Together, you create more love than either could generate alone.

We can only meet another as deeply as we've met ourselves and that is the deepest teaching of self-love. We can only love another as fully as we love ourselves. We can only allow intimacy to the degree we've become intimate with our own being.

This means bringing our imperfect, growing, learning selves to connection with consciousness and care. It means taking responsibility for our own healing while allowing another to witness and support. It means loving ourselves enough to choose partners who celebrate our wholeness rather than needing our brokenness.

Relationships are mirrors, teachers, catalysts for growth. But they are not your source of worth, you are. The love you cultivate within is the love you bring to connection. The wholeness you claim is the wholeness you share.

In this work, there is the opportunity of loving yourself so fully that you transform every relationship you touch, becoming a beacon of what's possible when someone chooses themselves while also choosing connection. The world needs this. We need people who can love without losing themselves. The world needs the medicine of conscious connection: practicing the sacred art of loving ourselves while loving others.

Return your hands to your heart. Feel your own pulse, your own presence, your own wholeness. You are complete. And from this completeness, you can love in ways that heal, that inspire, that transform. This is self-love in relationship. This is love as spiritual practice. This is you, choosing yourself while choosing to love.

9

BECOMING YOUR OWN BELOVED

Close your eyes and imagine standing at the threshold of the most important ceremony of your life. You're dressed in whatever makes you feel most radiant. Candles flicker around you. The air holds that particular quality of sacred anticipation. But here's the revelation: you're not waiting for someone to arrive. You're not hoping to be chosen. The beloved you're about to commit to is already here, has always been here. Place your hand on your heart. Feel that faithful beat. The beloved is you.

There comes a moment in every love story when the gesture must be made, the ring offered, the vow spoken, the commitment declared. In our journey of self-love, this moment arrives not with fanfare but with quiet recognition: I choose you. Not someday when you're perfect. Not if you meet certain conditions. But now, as you are, in all your becoming.

To become your own beloved is to stop waiting for external salvation. Look yourself in the mirror, look into your eyes, and realise that the love you've been seeking in every face, every embrace, every validation, has been living inside you all along, not as potential but as presence, waiting to be claimed.

The Myth That Keeps Us Seeking

Our culture is obsessed with the idea of finding "the one", our soulmate, our better half, our missing piece. From fairy tales to dating apps, we're taught that true happiness comes from being chosen by another, that romantic love is the ultimate goal, that we're incomplete until we're coupled.

I lived this myth for years, staring at partners hoping to see myself as whole, valuable, enough. I would pour everything into relationships, weaving unconscious spells of projection, trying to drink from another what I was dying of thirst for in myself. But this seeking outside ourselves is not just futile, it's a form of self-abandonment. We're giving others an impossible job: to convince us of what we refuse to believe ourselves. We're making them responsible for what only we can provide: the unconditional acceptance of our own being.

Carl Jung wrote extensively about the hieros gamos, the sacred marriage within. This mystical union isn't simply a psychological concept, it's a spiritual milestone in the journey towards wholeness. It's the marriage of all our opposites: our darkness and light, our masculine and feminine, our human and divine. It's becoming whole within ourselves so that outer relationships become celebrations rather than desperate salvations.

This is not a way to bypass genuine human connection. We must avoid the temptation to protect ourselves behind a fortress of "I don't need anyone." Underneath this lives the unhealed wound of disappointment in human connection. Sometimes, being single is an excellent choice, yes, but connection of various kinds is so important. Human beings are social and communal animals, and in order to do the deepest healing, we sometimes need a trusted sacred mirror rather than avoid the vulnerability of intimacy. Try to avoid:

- Using "I love myself" to avoid the risk of loving others
- Spiritual bypassing that denies legitimate needs for partnership
- Becoming so self-contained that we lose the capacity for deep connection
- Confusing self-love with narcissism or self-obsession
- Escaping into a perfect inner world so that the outer world feels unnecessary

No, this work is not about avoiding others. It means being whole AND acknowledging that wholeness includes the capacity for connection, the desire for witness, the longing to share our one wild and precious life.

As Buddhist teacher Tara Brach reminds us, "The boundary to what we can accept is the boundary to our freedom." This includes accepting our need for others even as we commit to ourselves.

When Life Brings You to Your Knees

Let's talk about what happens to being your own beloved when life shatters you; When depression descends like fog and you can barely remember your name, let alone your vow to love yourself; When grief hollows you out until you're echo and absence; When illness or trauma makes your body feel like enemy territory again.

I learned this during a particularly brutal depression following multiple losses. All my beautiful self-love practices felt like mockery. How could I be love myself when I could barely stand to exist? The affirmations I'd spoken felt like lies.

The commitment here is for better and for worse. It isn't to just love yourself when you're shining, it's to stay present through all seasons. Sometimes being your own beloved looks like:

- Calling a friend or asking for a hug when you can't hold yourself
- Taking medication because that's how you love your struggling brain
- Letting yourself fall apart and grieving openly without adding shame to the pain
- Understanding that asking for help IS an act of self-love

Francis Weller, who writes about communal grief, says, "The work of the mature person is to carry grief in one hand and gratitude in the other and to be stretched large by them." In this work, we are stretching ourselves to be enough to hold both the beauty of self-love and the devastation of being human.

We are not self-contained units. We are interconnected beings who literally co-regulate with others. Our nervous systems sync up. Dr. Sue Johnson, who developed Emotionally Focused Therapy, emphasises that we are "bonding mammals" who need secure connection for optimal functioning. Being your own beloved doesn't eliminate this need, it transforms how we meet it.

Don't forget that in this work we are not seeking someone to complete us; we are looking for companions for the journey rather than saviours; co-creators rather than projections screens; and fellow travellers rather than destinations. Just as the mystic poet Rainer Maria Rilke wrote,

> "Love consists in this: two solitudes that
> meet, protect and greet each other."

This work doesn't banish the inner critic, that voice that catalogues your failures, that echoed unworthiness; it doesn't simply vanish in the light of self-love. What changes is your relationship to it. When the critic speaks, you might respond differently:

Old response: "You're right, I'm worthless." New response: "I hear you're scared. What do you need?"

Old response: Believing every harsh word. New response: "Thank you for trying to protect me, but I've got this."

Old response: Days of shame spiral. New response: "Even with this criticism present, I choose myself."

The inner critic becomes like a worried relative at your wedding, present, perhaps annoying, but no longer running the show. You might even develop affection for this part that tried so hard to keep you safe through criticism.

The Mythic Mirror: Descent as the Path to Inner Marriage

In stories of love, the beloved tends always to be elsewhere, outside of ourselves, hidden in a distant kingdom. The princess is sleeping in a tower, perhaps guarded by dragons. The hero must journey outward, conquer obstacles, prove their worth to win the prize of love. But there are older deeper stories where the transformation isn't found through conquest but through descent, not through seeking outside but through surrendering to the journey within.

The story of Psyche, whose name means soul, is over two thousand years old. Psyche is the most beautiful mortal woman, so lovely that people worship her over Aphrodite. She's married to Eros, a god she's forbidden to see, living in paradise but in darkness, loved but not truly known. This is how many of us live, disconnected, so that even if we are partnered we do not feel truly seen.

When Psyche lights her lamp to see Eros, she chooses knowledge over safety and loses everything. Cast out, pregnant, abandoned, she must complete four impossible tasks to earn reunion with her beloved. She doesn't complete them through force or cleverness. She completes them by listening to the smallest voices.

When told to sort an enormous pile of mixed grains before dawn, she despairs. But the ants come, the tiniest, most overlooked creatures, and sort grain by grain through the night. When sent to gather golden fleece from murderous rams, the river reeds whisper: wait until noon when they sleep, then gather wool caught on the branches. When commanded to fill a flask from the Styx, an eagle appears to help. Even her final task, to journey to the underworld for Persephone's beauty cream, succeeds only when she listens to the tower's advice.

Psyche reunites with love not through heroic action but through accepting help from the overlooked, the tiny, the rejected. The ants are our small daily practices. The reeds are our intuition's wisdom. The eagle is our broader perspective. The tower is the inner knowing of how to navigate the dark.

There's a deeper teaching here. Psyche's real journey isn't to win back Eros, it's to become divine herself. Through her tasks, through her descent, she transforms from mortal to goddess. She doesn't just reunite with her beloved; she becomes her own divine eternal self. The outer was always just the catalyst for the inner transformation.

This echoes the mythos of Inanna, one of the oldest stories known to humanity. The Sumerian goddess, queen of heaven and earth, descends to the underworld to face the dark goddess, Ereshkigal. At each of seven gates, Inanna is stripped of a piece of her royal regalia; her crown, her jewellery, her armour, her robes. She who was queen of heaven enters the underworld naked, stripped of every external marker of worth.

In this bare, vulnerable way, she faces the terror of the unknown, and her own death. Yes, Ereshkigal kills her. For three days, Inanna hangs on a hook, in limbo. The goddess who had everything experiences having nothing, being nothing. Inanna, in her wisdom, had a backup plan. Her faithful servant follows her pre-arranged instructions and goes to the other gods for help. Only Enki, god of wisdom and water, responds. Enki doesn't send warriors or use force. He takes dirt from under his fingernails and creates two tiny beings, so small they can slip through the cracks of the underworld's gates.

When they reach the throne room, they find Ereshkigal, not in triumph, but in agony. She's moaning in pain. The creatures don't try to fix or fight. They simply mirror her pain back to her. When she cries "Oh! My heart!" they cry "Oh! Your heart!" They witness her pain without trying to change it, judge it, or take it away. This simple act of empathetic witnessing transforms everything. For perhaps the first time ever, the Queen of the Underworld feels seen in her suffering. So too, do our shadows need to be seen.

Moved by this compassion, Ereshkigal offers them any gift. They ask only for the corpse hanging on the hook. She agrees. The beings sprinkle the food and water of life on Inanna. Inanna rises, not freed by force or divine decree, but because someone witnessed suffering without trying to fix it. The magic was in the empathy that made Ereshkigal willing to release what she held.

This is why, in trauma work, in shadow work, in any deep healing, the witnessing is the medicine. Not fixing. Not fighting. But saying to our own wounded parts: "Oh, your heart. Oh, your pain. I see. I'm here with you in this."

This simple witnessing of pain releases Inanna to return. But she returns changed. She who descended as Queen of Heaven alone returns with Ereshkigal's demons as companions. She who knew only the upper world now knows the depths. She who was only light now carries darkness too. She is whole.

This is our journey. To become our own beloved, we must descend, stripping away every external thing we thought made us worthy: accomplishments, roles, carefully constructed identity. We must face our own dark sister, the rejected parts, the shadow self who was cast into the underworld of unconscious.

In that underworld, we pause. We feel the death of we thought we were; the pretty stories we told ourselves about yourself rot away. This composting is important. We meet our own Ereshkigal, the parts that rage, that grieve, that were cast out for being too much, too scary, too real.

And in the meeting, in the witnessing, transformation begins.

The ants that help us might be daily practice of affirmations, sorting through the mixed messages grain by grain, separating nourishment from poison. The reeds might be the voice of our intuition or of dear friends or good therapists, telling us how to gather what we need. The eagle might be that moment of perspective when we see our lives from above. The tower might be tuning in to the wisdom of our bodies. The beings that come to help might be our journals or mirror work, witnessing our pain without trying to fix it.

In encountering these transformative journeys, you are Psyche lighting the lamp, choosing to see clearly even if it costs you everything. You are Inanna. You are both the one who descends and the one who rises. You are the seeker and the sought, the lover and the beloved, the one who dies to false self and the one reborn in truth, who dies to the past to be reborn in the present as the old Zen saying goes.

The return is different than we imagined. Psyche returns with new life and becomes immortal. Inanna returns with the demons as her companions, integrated rather than banished, stronger than ever and ready to re-claim her throne. You return from your descent more whole, knowing yourself at a deeper level. Every death of false self makes space for true self to emerge. In this work, you choose yourself, again and again, at each gate, in each descent, through each dark night, until you emerge carrying both divine light and underworld wisdom.

The Bridge to Service

Surprisingly, loving myself has made me more available for service to others, not less. When you're not desperately seeking love, you have more love to give. When you're not looking for salvation, you can offer support. When you know you're whole, you can help others remember their own wholeness.

Self-love naturally overflows. The love you cultivate for yourself becomes love available for the world. But it's service from wholeness rather than depletion, giving from abundance rather than deficit.

When you're truly your own beloved, dating and relationships transform. You're no longer auditioning for the role of chosen one. You're not performing for approval. You're showing up as yourself, curious about connection but not desperate for it.

This can be disorienting for others. People are used to being needed in that desperate way. They might feel rejected by your wholeness. They might try to create dependency. They might be attracted to your self-love but then threatened by it.

When you say "I won't abandon myself for relationship." Some people might run. Others might be intrigued. As you do in this work, partners might feel displaced until they realise they're getting more of you, not less.

This Is Just the Beginning

The inner marriage is a doorway. On the other side lies a life where self-love isn't something you practice but something you embody. Where every experience becomes an opportunity to deepen this primary relationship with yourself. Where you meet the world as one who knows they are loved from the inside out.

But it's not a transcendent state that lifts you above human struggle. It's a grounded practice that helps you meet struggle with more grace. You'll still feel lonely sometimes. You'll still long for connection, because that's human, but you'll also be on the path to connecting more deeply and in more satisfying ways. You'll still wrestle with shadows and critic voices and the sometimes brutal reality of being human.

You won't be alone in that wrestling. You'll have yourself, not as concept but as lived experience. The inner-beloved who says, "I'm here with you through all of it."

As we close this journey together, let's honour what you've done. You've walked the hero's path of self-reclamation. You've descended into shadow and returned with medicine. You've reclaimed your exiled light. You've come home to your body. You've learned the sacred art of boundaries. You've transformed how you love.

And now, you stand at the threshold of the deepest commitment, to be your own beloved through all of life's seasons.

This doesn't mean you're finished. The path continues. You'll meet new edges, new shadows, deeper layers of light. But now you walk as one who has remembered the most essential thing: you belong to yourself. You are worthy of your own devotion. You are the love you've been seeking.

The world needs people who love themselves this deeply, not from the disconnection of narcissism but from wholeness.

A Final Blessing and Beginning

Return to the mirror. But this time, see everything, your humanity and divinity, your struggles and strength, your shadows and light. See the journey you've walked. The courage it took. The love you've cultivated.

Place both hands over your heart. Feel that faithful rhythm, the beat that has carried you through everything and will carry you through whatever comes.

Speak these words, or let your own arise:

"I see you, all of you, all of us, and I choose us.

Not despite our flaws but including them.

Not when we're perfect but as we are.

I vow to stay present through all seasons.

To return when I drift.

To ask for help when I cannot hold myself.

To celebrate our becoming.

To honour our humanity.

To trust our divinity.

I am my beloved.

This is my promise. This is my practice.

Forever and always, as long as we both shall live."

Let your hands fall. Turn from the mirror. Walk into your life knowing:

The beloved walks with you.

The beloved breathes through you.

The beloved lives as you.

You are married to the mystery of your own becoming in sacred union. You are wed to life itself. You are allowing yourself to be the one you've been waiting for.

Welcome home, beloved. Welcome to a new beginning.

CONCLUSION: THE RETURN

Once upon a time, there was a soul who forgot they were whole. They wandered through dark forests of self-doubt, climbed mountains of perfectionism, and nearly drowned in rivers of other people's expectations. They sought the magic in everyone else's eyes, never knowing it lived in their own bones all along. This soul, dear reader, was you. And now, at the end of this tale that is really a beginning, you have become both the hero and the treasure, the seeker and the found, the lover and the beloved.

We have travelled far together. Through nine chapters, nine initiations, nine territories of becoming. Each one has been a doorway, and you have walked through them all, sometimes with confidence, sometimes crawling, but always moving toward the truth of your own wholeness.

Let us pause here, at the threshold between ending and beginning, to honour the journey you've taken.

The Fairy Tale Was Always Yours

As we touched on at the beginning, every fairy tale you've ever heard, every myth that stirred your soul, was always about this journey you've just completed. But not in the way you were taught to read them. As Clarissa Pinkola Estés reveals: we are every character in the story. The fairy tale isn't about external events, it's the map of our inner world, the chronicle of psyche becoming whole.

In Sleeping Beauty, the whole kingdom falls asleep, not just the princess but everyone, frozen in time. This is what happens when we abandon ourselves: every part of our psyche slumbers under the spell. The thorns that grow around the castle are the defences we build. We need to connect with our inner champion who finally breaks through, because we are the only one who truly has that power, not someone outside ourselves but the part of us finally ready to wake, to push through our own protective thorns and kiss our sleeping self back to life.

We are both Beauty and Beast, the part that can see with the eyes of love and the part that feels monstrous, unlovable, exiled. The transformation happens not when someone else finally loves your beastly aspects but when you stay present with what seems ugly and frightening in yourself long enough to see its hidden nobility.

Cinderella isn't saved by a prince. In the oldest versions, she speaks to her dead mother through a tree, she connects to her ancestral wisdom, her inner knowing. The fairy godmother is her own deeper magic awakening. The prince who recognises her is the part of herself that sees past all disguises to her true worth. The whole tale is about remembering who you are beneath the ashes of conditioning.

In every mythological journey, the hero must return home transformed, bringing treasure and medicine to heal and replenish. When you understand the inner nature of the tale, you realise you are the hero, the home, the treasure, and the barren land ready and waiting to bloom again.

Your treasure is your reclaimed wholeness, with every shadow you integrate, every light uncovered, every boundary learned, every part of yourself brought home to the wedding feast. There will still be droughts and barren lands within, anywhere you still believe the lie of unworthiness, any relationship still based on self-abandonment, any moment you forget you are already whole.

The hero's return isn't in going back to who you were; it's in moving forward as who you've become.

Letters to Love

Many years ago, the writer Elizabeth Gilbert began a practice of writing letters to Love itself.

Each morning, she would write: "Dear Love, what would you have me know today?" Then, she would wait and let Love write back.

What emerged astonished her. Love's voice was infinitely patient, endlessly kind, seeing her wholeness even when she couldn't. Love would write: "Dear Child, you think you need to earn me, but I am already here. You think you need to be perfect to deserve me, but I love your imperfection most of all. You think you are separate from me, but you are made of me."

This practice embodies everything we've explored. When you write to Love and let Love write back, you're doing what fairy tales have always taught: recognising that the magic lives inside you. You're discovering that the beloved you've been seeking has been trying to reach you all along.

In this kind of practice we too can find that Love has been writing to us all along, in every kindness from a stranger, every moment of beauty, every time we choose ourselves, even slightly. The practice simply makes us available to receive what was always being transmitted.

The Never-Ending Story

The fairy tale doesn't end with "happily ever after", that's a mistranslation that has caused much suffering. The old stories say "they lived happily in the ever after." In the ever-evolving journey of the inner psyche and collective consciousness where story dwells.

Your story continues. The path spirals in and out which means you'll meet these teachings again at deeper levels. At forty, sixty, eighty, you might meet shadows you thought were integrated. You might discover new golden light hidden even deeper. Your body might need different tending through illness or aging. Your boundaries might need adjusting as life changes. Your inner marriage might need renewal through loss or transformation.

This is the nature of being human. We forget and remember, lose ourselves and return, abandon and reclaim, over and over. But each spiral teaches something new. Each return is swifter. Each remembering goes deeper.

The child who first learned unworthiness is still within you, but now you know how to hold them. The critic who protected through cruelty is still there, but now you can dialogue with love. The shadows still arise, but now you greet them as teachers. The light still sometimes feels too bright, but now you know it's yours to shine.

You Are the Living Fairy Tale

As you close this book, you're not ending but beginning. You've become a living fairy tale, proof that transformation is possible, that spells can be broken, that we can gather our bones and sing them back to life.

Your very existence now challenges the dominant story. Every time you approve of yourself without conditions, you disrupt industries built on inadequacy. Every time you honour your shadows with curiosity instead of shame, you model a new way of being human. Every time you choose yourself while also choosing connection, you pioneer conscious relationship.

In this work, we become what the world desperately needs: people who know love from the inside out. Our self-love isn't selfish, it's medicine for a culture dying of self-hatred. Our wholeness gives others permission to seek their own. Our integrated shadows show others that darkness isn't evil but human. Our shining light reminds others they're allowed to be brilliant.

So here, at the end that is the beginning, let us speak the deepest truth: We are the ones we've been waiting for. We always have been. We always will be.

Not because we've perfected ourselves, because being perfect really isn't a natural state within life, it tends to be an unreasonable expectation unless we can appreciate the perfection hidden in plain sight – imbedded in the messy complex imperfection of life. The truth is:

The love you seek lives within you.

The magic you want is in your bones.

The home you long for is your own heart.

The beloved you await is reading these words right now.

Every spiritual tradition has tried to tell us this. Every fairy tale has encoded it. Every myth has mapped the journey. But we had to walk it ourselves, through our own shadows and light, our own abandonment and return, to really know it as living truth.

And So It Continues

Once upon a time, which is now, there was a soul who remembered they were whole. Through great trials and deep magic, through shadow work and light reclaiming, through body wisdom and boundary teaching, through the sacred art of self-approval and the daily practice of devotion, they came home to themselves.

That soul, dear one, is you.

You are the fairy tale and its resolution. You are the journey and the destination. You are the magic spell and the one who breaks it. You are the sleeping beauty and the awakening kiss. You are the beast and the one who sees beauty. You are the lost child and the breadcrumbs and the home.

The wicked witch was also the wise woman, you've integrated her power.

The poisoned apple was also the catalyst, you've thanked it for waking you.

The dark forest was also the sacred grove, you've learned from its shadows.

The locked tower was also the sanctuary, you've honoured your need for boundaries.

The dragon guarding treasure was your own fierce protection, you've reclaimed your fire.

Now you know: every fairy tale is your story. Every character is your teacher. Every ending is your beginning.

The path continues, but you walk it now with different eyes. You see the magic hidden in plain sight. You know the beloved in every mirror. You trust the journey even when you can't see the destination.

This is your happily in the ever after, a powerful present where you choose yourself again and again. Now, love isn't something you seek but something you are.

Welcome home, beloved. You belong here.

EXTRAS

Self-love reading meditation

Soften your gaze. Feel your body as it is, right here. Let yourself be held by gravity, the way the earth quietly holds every living thing. Notice the gentle weight in your limbs, the quiet warmth in your hands, the simple fact that you are here.

Let your breath come and go without any effort. With each exhale, imagine a little more of the tension draining out of you. Feel the muscles of your face loosening, your jaw unhooking, your shoulders dropping a fraction closer to ease.

As you soften, there is nothing to do and nothing to get right. You don't need to achieve anything. Simply notice that you are already breathing, already sensing, already aware. The moment is here, and you are part of it.

Allow whatever you feel to be just as it is. Even the tightness or the fidgeting or the thoughts. Instead of resisting, imagine opening a window inside yourself and letting fresh air move through every corner. You can be the space that holds everything.

Notice the subtle sense of life moving through you, the tingling under your skin, the pulsing of your heart. This is presence. This is aliveness. Nothing extra is required.

If you like, you can quietly affirm to yourself: I am here. I am willing to soften. I am open to experience.

Feel your body as it is, right here. Let yourself be held by gravity, the way the earth quietly holds every living thing. Notice the gentle weight in your limbs, the quiet warmth in your hands, the simple fact that you are here.

Let your breath come and go without any effort. With each exhale, imagine a little more of the tension draining out of you. Feel the muscles of your face loosening, your jaw unhooking, your shoulders dropping a fraction closer to ease.

As you soften, there is nothing to do and nothing to get right. You don't need to achieve anything. Simply notice that you are already breathing, already sensing, already aware. The moment is here, and you are part of it.

Allow whatever you feel to be just as it is. Even the tightness or the fidgeting or the thoughts. Instead of resisting, imagine opening a window inside yourself and letting fresh air move through every corner. You can be the space that holds everything.

Notice the subtle sense of life moving through you, the tingling under your skin, the pulsing of your heart. This is presence. This is aliveness. Nothing extra is required.

If you like, you can quietly affirm to yourself: I am here. I am willing to soften. I am open to experience.

Stay here as long as you wish. Whenever you're ready, gently bring your awareness back, carrying this softness into whatever comes next.

Sacred union ritual

Something ancient awakens when you decide to marry yourself. The old gods smile. The ancestors lean in. Honour this rite of claiming yourself as sacred, of speaking vows into the void and hearing them echo back as truth.

You are about to perform one of the oldest spells there is: making the invisible visible, calling form from formlessness, speaking yourself into a new reality. This is threshold magic. Crossroads work. The kind of ceremony that changes the pattern in the weave of things.

Magic requires containers. Begin gathering what will hold your intention:

Water - for the emotions that will move, for cleansing what was, for blessing what comes. Collect it from rain, tears, the sea, or bless tap water with salt.

Fire - for transformation, for burning what must die, for lighting the way forward. You will need a lighter or matches, or, if you aren't able to use real fire, you can imagine this part. Choose candles that make sense for you: White for beginning? Red for passion? Black for the mystery of union?

Earth - something to ground this work in the physical: stones you've gathered from nature, crystals you already have around your home. If you have houseplants, you can arrange them around the space for your ritual. You could also gather flowers to honour yourself with. You will need some food too, to ground you at the end of the ritual. Choose something that is special to you, even if that's just a piece of your favourite chocolate.

Air - incense or a bundle of herbs to carry your words between worlds. Choose cleansing sage, juniper, cedar or any incense that speaks to you.

The Mirror - for seeing through the surface to the truth of yourself. This will be your witness.

The Token – choose a token that will carry this spell forward? A ring to remind you of your commitment to return to self? A special stone for grounding? A pendant that rests against your heart? Choose what your body wants to carry.

The Words – paper and pen to write your vows like you're writing incantations for your new reality. Consider: what do you want to vow to yourself? What vows would you like to receive from your past self? How can you honour yourself with vows? You may want to write these vows before the ritual, taking time with them, or you may prefer to write them as part of the process, whatever feels right to you.

The Cleansing, Blessing and Creating Sacred Space

Take your water and anoint yourself:

Feet: I cleanse the paths I walked away from myself.

Hands: I cleanse the reaching for salvation in others.

Heart: I cleanse the betrayals I committed against my own knowing.

Throat: I cleanse the words I swallowed, the truths I didn't speak.

Forehead: I cleanse the illusions I preferred to my own sight.

Crown: I cleanse the disconnection from my own divinity.

Let the water wake up every cell to what's happening.

Sprinkle water around your space and say something like:

Element of water, bearer of life. With your power, I cleanse and bless this space. I honour the waters of my being, the flow that knows its way home.

Light your incense and waft the smoke around the space:

With the element of air, I bless this space. I call to my breath, my words, the space between in and out where magic lives.

Light your candles:

I call to the flame within me, the spark that survives all storms.

Place your earth elements down on the ground, arranging them:

I call to my bones, my flesh, the sacred matter that makes me real.

Stand in the centre of what you've created. Feel the circle of your own presence extending out like ripples. You need no other permission than your own intention. You are the priestess of this rite. You are the temple and the divine being honoured.

This is sacred time. This is sacred space. I am fully present, here and now.

The Summoning

Close your eyes and call yourself present. Not just the you standing there but all the past yous you've been:

I call to the child who knew my magic before the world taught doubt.

I call to the child who gave my power away for love.

I call to the one who forgot, while trying to be everything.

I call to the crone already living in my bones, holding tomorrow's wisdom.

I call to the shadow selves, the golden selves, the abandoned selves.

I call to the witch who remembers, the wise one, the powerful self who commands presence, the wild one who runs with the Moon and tides.

Come. Gather. We are making ourselves whole.

Feel them coming. The circle fills with all your possibilities, your powers, your archetypes, your past selves. They are all here to witness this union.

The Descent and Return

Sit before your mirror. Look past the surface you've learned to judge. Past the masks. Look until you see the deeper one looking back, ancient, immortal, wearing your face like a garment.

Speak to what you see:

I know you. You who were here before the wounding. You who will be here after the healing. You who exist outside the story, inside the story, as the story itself. I see you.

Now close your eyes and drop deeper. Down through layers of self, through the sediment of years, until you reach the bottom of your own well. Here lives the one you came to love, not perfect but utterly, devastatingly real.

In this deep place, let the sacred union of self-marriage happen first in the imaginal realm. See yourself taking your own hands. See yourself speaking promises that rewrite the laws of your universe. See yourself placing the ring, the kiss, the blessing. What happens in the depths is real. What happens in the imaginal creates the possible.

The Sacred Vows

Open your eyes. Light incense again from your candle flame, joining fire and air. If you've pre-written vows, this is the time to read them. If you prefer the vows to come to you now, write them down so that you are making them a tangible reminder that you can come back to over the next days, weeks, months and years, as a touchstone.

As the smoke rises, look yourself in the mirror and speak your vows into the spiralling smoke.

Let them be spell, promise, and creation:

By my will and my word, I take myself as beloved.

You may also like to include some of the following:

I vow to seek myself when I go missing, to sing myself back from the deadlands of others' expectations.

I vow to be the guardian at my own gates, letting in only what serves, letting out only what's true.

I vow to bravely face my shadows under every moon, to shine my light without apology under the light of the sun.

I claim my magic: messy, imperfect, mine. I claim my knowing: body and soul, bone-deep, beyond question.

I unite with the wise one within me who remembers the old ways. I unite with the child who still believes in wonder. I unite with the crone who laughs at what cannot touch my essence.

By root and bone, by blood and breath, by the spiral of return that brings all things home, I am my own. I am whole. I am committed to the mystery of my own becoming.

I belong to myself before I belong to any other. I am sovereign. I am claimed. I am home.

So it is spoken. So it is done.

Take your token in your left hand, receive with your right.

Sprinkle it with water: By water, cleansed.

Pass it through the incense smoke: By air, blessed.

Pass it over the candle flame: By fire, transformed.

Touch it to a stone you have gathered and then to your heart: By earth, made real.

Hold it to your heart a few moments longer. Feel your heartbeat charging it with your life force.

Place your token on your body knowing that the spell is sealed.

The Sacred Feast

Magic requires grounding. As you eat, you nourish your magic. You make real what you have spoken.

This is both grounding and more deeply connecting with how magic moves from the ethereal to the physical, through the body, through pleasure, through the sacred act of taking the world into yourself and making it part of you.

Closing the Circle

Stand in your sacred space one last time as a newly united being. Thank the elements:

Flame, thank you for witnessing. May I carry your transformation.

Water, thank you for cleansing. May I flow with my own truth.

Earth, thank you for grounding. May I remain grounded in my power.

Air, thank you for carrying. May my words create reality.

Thank the selves who gathered: We are united. We are one. We are free.

Blow out your candles knowing the light continues within. Pour your water to the earth or save it for future magic. Keep something from this circle along with your vows: ash, wax, a stone, a flower, to remind you.

You have spoken yourself into a new reality, but magic requires tending. Each time you touch your token, the spell reinforces. Each time you choose yourself, the magic deepens. Each time you return from a disconnection with yourself, the reconnection strengthens the bond.

You may choose to renew your vows from time to time, whenever it feels right: On the full moon, or the dark moon, on your birthday. In crisis, remember: you are committed to yourself and that union is stronger than any storm.

You have claimed yourself in the circle. You have spoken the words that create worlds. The magic is not that you'll never struggle, the magic is that you'll never again be alone in the struggle. You are your own beloved.

The spell is cast. The rite is complete. The magic continues.

SELF LOVE MAGIC, THE COURSE!

If you want to go deeper into the magic of self-love…
I've created this course with you in mind.

https://irisbeaglehole.com/b/self-love-magic

Four thoughtfully designed modules to inspire a gentle, powerful return to self:

. . .

THE OPENING

Lay the foundation with simple, sacred practices that begin to shift your inner dialogue. You'll meet yourself with softness, honesty, and a willingness to begin again.

The Undoing

Gently unlearn the harmful labels and beliefs you've inherited. Through affirmation, journaling, and guided meditation, you'll start to rewrite your story.

Reclaiming & Embodying

Turn toward your body with reverence. These sessions support you to reconnect with the parts of you that shine and have been silenced.

The Integration

Create your own self-love ritual, reflect on your growth, and step forward with devotion. This is where practice becomes presence and self-love becomes a way of being.

AWAKENING THE WILD WITCH

"To me, being a witch is about connecting with nature, appreciating all of the sensations of life, opening up to the vastness and beautiful complexity of experience, and stepping into our power..."

IRIS BEAGLEHOLE, author of the Myrtlewood Mysteries, invites you to awaken the wild and delightful magic within. This enchanting guide blends humour, heart, and wisdom to lead you on a transformative journey of self-discovery and empowerment. Whether you are new to the path of witchcraft or a seasoned practitioner, Awakening the Wild Witch will help you claim your power and awaken further to your own wild magic.

~ TAP into the innate magic that resides within you by connecting deeply with your intuition and the wisdom of your body.

~ Create meaningful rituals, craft ceremonies and spellwork and embrace change with grace and intention.

~ Work with the elements, harness the power of the natural world, and align with the rhythms of nature.

~ Deepen your understanding of magical herbs, crystals, astrology and kitchen witchery.

~ Explore the powerful potential of your shadow, delve into the depths of your psyche to heal and empower yourself, transforming shadows into sources of strength and insight.

AWAKENING *the Wild Witch is an invitation to step into your wild magic and embrace the vast possibilities that lie within you. With practical exercises, rituals, and meditations, Iris invites you on this journey of deepening awareness and opening to a life filled with wild magic, purpose, and inspiration.*

. . .

AVAILABLE IN EBOOK, *paperback, hardback. Note that the gorgeous deluxe hardback editions are only available through my website*

CHECK OUT IRIS'S MAGICAL FICTION

Myrtlewood Mysteries (9 books)

Rosemary Thorn and her teen daughter Athena move to the quirky, magical town of Myrtlewood, confronting grief, identity and the ups and downs of maternal tension. In *Accidental Magic*, Rosemary rediscovers her inherited power and begins healing from her past. Through late spring in *Experimental Magic* and Beltane in *Combustible Magic*, Athena awakens to her own magic, asserting identity and autonomy. *Celestial Magic* explores their evolving mother-daughter bond and how trust shapes growth. Each instalment offers seasonal rites that mirror deeper self-trust, emotional courage and letting go.

Myrtlewood Crones (5 so far)

Centered on older witches reclaiming power, community and purpose with plenty of sassy banter! Embracing the power of the wise woman archetype, mature witches reclaim their magic and power. It's a loving reminder that our inner fire only grows stronger with age and self-trust. As they learn to honour their experience, readers witness self-worth maturing like fine whiskey—age as strength, not loss and havign something to look forward to as we age!

DREAMREALM MYSTERIES (3 books)

A young Dreamweaver, Awa, travels through lucid dreamscapes learning how to cope with anxiety, face challenges and heal. In this trilogy, suitable for ages 9-99, each book follows inner and outer-world quests: facing hidden fears, integrating shadow and light, and alchemising into empowerment.

KOTAHI BAY (CO-WRITTEN with Nova Blake)

In *In the Spirit* and *In the Earth's Embrace*, Alyssa inherits earth-linked magic, reconnecting with ancestral land and identity. Through ceremony and earth healing, she reclaims belonging, roots, and trust in herself—a soulful mirror for grounding self-love.

THE WITCHES of Holloway Road (Standalone)

Ursula, newly heartbroken, discovers her own craft and resilience. Her journey is one of inner reclamation: from fear of vulnerability to embracing strength, facing her shadow, building self-trust and choosing joy beyond pain.

SELECTED RESOURCES

Louise Hay - *You Can Heal Your Life* (1984)
Michael Norton - *The Ritual Effect* (2024)
Sonya Renee Taylor - *The Body is Not an Apology* (2018)
Hillary McBride - *The Wisdom of Your Body* (2021)
Emily Nagoski - *Come As You Are* (2015)
Kasia Urbaniak - *Unbound* (2021)
Christy Harrison - *Anti-Diet* (2019)
Clarissa Pinkola Estés - *Women Who Run With the Wolves* (1992)
Brené Brown - *The Gifts of Imperfection* (2010)
Richard Schwartz - *No Bad Parts* (2021)
Bessel van der Kolk - *The Body Keeps the Score* (2014)
Donald Winnicott - *Playing and Reality* (1971)
Stan Tatkin - *Wired for Love* (2012)
Terry Real - *Getting Past You and Me to Build a More Loving Relationship* (2022)
Harville Hendrix - *Getting the Love You Want* (1988)
Sue Johnson - *Hold Me Tight* (2008)

Deb Dana - *Anchored: How to Befriend Your Nervous System Using Polyvagal Theory* (2021)

Peter Levine - *Waking the Tiger: Healing Trauma* (1997); *In an Unspoken Voice* (2010)

Audre Lorde - *Sister Outsider* (1984)

bell hooks - *All About Love: New Visions* (2000)

Tara Brach - *Radical Acceptance* (2004)

Francis Weller - *The Wild Edge of Sorrow: Rituals of Renewal and the Sacred Work of Grief* (2015)

John O'Donohue - *Anam Cara: A Book of Celtic Wisdom* (1997)

Mary Oliver - *Devotions* (2017)

Elizabeth Gilbert - *Big Magic: Creative Living Beyond Fear* (2015)

Roxane Gay - *Hunger: A Memoir of (My) Body* (2017); Sarah Baldwin's *You Make Sense* (podcast)

Resmaa Menakem - *My Grandmother's Hands* (2017)

Esther Perel - *Mating in Captivity* (2006);

Dr. Nadine Burke Harris - *The Deepest Well: Healing the Long-Term Effects of Childhood Trauma and Adversity*

ACKNOWLEDGMENTS

This book exists in part because of the many souls who have walked beside me on this winding path toward wholeness.

To every reader who recognises their own story in these words: you are not alone in this journey home to yourself.

My deepest gratitude to Mary, who first placed Louise Hay's transformative work in my hands all those years ago in her rose garden. To Louise Hay herself, whose work and radical self-love teachings planted seeds that still bloom in these pages. To Clarissa Pinkola Estés, whose bone-deep wisdom about story medicine gave me a map when I was lost in the forest.

To my mentor, Pamela Meekings-Stewart and the Grove of the Summer Stars for reminding me to listen to the wisdom of trees and tune into the magic and intuition of nature.

To Sherry, my wonderfully stroppy therapist, who pushed me to keep writing when I could barely get out of bed. To Fiona, who saw my shadows before I could name them and taught me they were teachers, not enemies. To my beloved great aunt Ruth Beaglehole, whose lifetime dedication to compassionate education ripples through every page about tending our inner children.

To GiGi Kent and Talia Marshall, for your sharp, supportive and challenging editorial feedback that made this book even better, and to my early readers who sent through your enthusiastic praise and gentle feedback.

To my dear friends Zoe, Stephanie, and Chantal, who have supported my journey over the years with such tenacity and grace, and to Emma for your deep love, care, inspiration and connection.

To my daughter, my greatest teacher, who shows me daily what it means to meet life with authentic presence.

And finally, to all the broken parts of me that I learned to love—thank you for waiting so patiently for me to remember that we were never broken at all, just human, just learning, just finding our way back to wholeness.

With infinite love and gratitude, Iris

Made in United States
Orlando, FL
24 November 2025